TANKS
in detail

Light Tank M5 & M5A1
STUART VI & M8 HMC

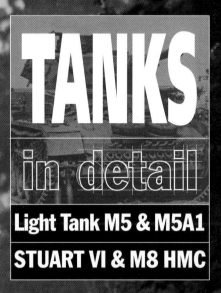

TANKS
in detail

Light Tank M5 & M5A1
STUART VI & M8 HMC

TERRY J. GANDER

Ian Allan
PUBLISHING

Acknowledgements

This book could not have been produced without
the invaluable assistance of the following people:
David Fletcher, Historian at the Tank Museum *(TM)*,
Bovington, Dorset, England; the Librarian Janice Taite and
the museum's photographer Roland Groom for original
images and prints from archive material. Thanks to John
Blackman for the colour photographs of restored tanks
and also to D P Dyer for the four-view drawings of the
M5/M5A1: to James D'eath for the M8 (HMC) drawings
and to Mike Rose for original colour artworks.

Jasper Spencer-Smith
Bournemouth, England
January 2004

Series Created & Edited by Jasper Spencer-Smith.
Design and Illustration: Nigel Pell.
Produced by JSS Publishing Limited,
Bournemouth, Dorset, England.

Title spread: An M5A1 of the US Army passes a knocked-out Tiger I in the
depths of the Bocage countryside in northern France around the time of the
Normandy landings in 1944. *(TM)*

First published 2004

ISBN 0 7110 3016 2

Published by Ian Allan Publishing

an imprint of Ian Allan Publishing Ltd, Hersham,
Surrey KT12 4RG.

Printed by Ian Allan Printing Ltd, Hersham,
Surrey KT12 4RG.

Code: 0406/A3

CONTENTS

CHAPTER ONE

DEVELOPMENT

The Light Tank M5 and M5A1 were the ultimate developments of the US light tank family that began with the M2 in the late 1930s. Of simple and sturdy design, this fast and reliable tank served extensively in several roles although it was no match against medium tanks.

The full story of the Light Tank M3, M3A1 and M3A3 is given in 'Tanks in Detail' No 2. Outlined in that account are the details of a series of standardised and hybrid vehicles that kept the US production lines manufacturing them in what seems to have been a permanent state of confusion as production changes and alternative components were introduced on an almost day-to-day basis. It became possible to detect at least 12 significant variants in the M3 series, while sub-marks and minor changes added more. For personnel in the field these many differences came to constitute a maintenance and spare parts supply problem. Perhaps the most problematic of those changes was caused by a perennial shortage of suitable engines.

When production of the Light Tank M3 series began the choice of the Wright Continental air-cooled radial petrol engine seemed to be correct. These engines were reliable, relatively light and delivered the required power. The main drawback to relying on radial engines came only when the US began to seriously prepare for the massive expansion in numbers and quantities of all manner of war matériel that World War Two was to demand.

The radial engines were primarily designed for aircraft. Once expansion of the US industrial war machine began to grow those engines became in great demand for their prime use, namely aircraft, and especially training aircraft. Some form of priority order had to be devised regarding the allocation of engines to the extent that at times the Light Tank M3 series production lines were in danger of grinding to a halt due to lack of suitable power plants. The provision of Guiberson diesel radial engines seemed to offer a viable alternative but in the event those M3 series vehicles provided with diesel installations were not accepted by the US armed forces as their introduction alongside petrol-driven radials would have caused too many maintenance and supply problems. Instead, the diesel-engined M3 models were sent abroad on Lend-Lease terms to the many nations that came to value them highly - the Soviet Union specified that tanks sent to them should have diesel engines whenever possible.

By the time the last major production model in the M3 series (the M3A3) was being produced, the engine supply problems had eased somewhat, mainly due to a major increase in engine production capacity achieved by the

Above:
Although marked as an M5 this vehicle is actually the pilot model, the M3E3, converted from an M3 series vehicle to test the new twin V-8 Cadillac engine installation. Note the two hull machine guns in the front (glacis) plate, one fixed (centrally) and the other on a flexible mounting. The fixed machine gun was soon deleted as being of little use in combat. *(TM)*

Left:
An early production Light Tank M5 undergoing trials, still featuring the two hull machine guns. *(TM)*

Above:
An overhead view of the M3E3 clearly showing the generous provision of access hatches for the crew in both the turret and hull roofs. Note the corner hinge arrangement of the hull hatches. Also note on the hull the pairs of fuel filling caps (outboard) and radiator filling caps (inboard). *(TM)*

Right:
The same vehicle as above but with all hatches closed, clearly showing the centrally-mounted fixed machine gun in the front (glacis) plate. *(TM)*

Above:
Driver training in a
Light Tank M5 with the
front two crew in the
preferred 'head-out'
position. Note that
this example does
not carry any machine
gun armament and
very little stowed
equipment. *(TM)*

allocation of new companies to the production programme. Yet the engine supply problems were not solved overnight and were to become an uncomfortable headache during Medium Tank M3 (Lee/Grant) and M4 (Sherman) production – see 'Tanks in Detail' Nos 4 and 6. However, as far as the Light Tanks were concerned a solution was in sight.

To facilitate the anticipated expansion in tank production in prospect by 1940, the US Ordnance Department had decided to call upon the nation's automotive industry to supplement the finite capabilities of the heavy engineering concerns originally intended to be involved in the mass production programmes. In practice that originally meant companies normally associated with locomotive and railway wagon production. As late as 1940 these companies were still greatly affected by the aftermath of the Great Depression years, during which the demand for railway products had largely fallen away. These companies therefore not only had the right type of manufacturing machinery to hand but they also had spare capacity that could be directed towards producing tanks.

Unfortunately for the Ordnance Department's plans it soon became apparent that the tank production demands had to be virtually doubled from what were already regarded as wildly ambitious and unprecedented totals. This was where the US automotive industry entered the scene. Once what few tanks that were available by then (June 1940) had been examined by automotive industry personnel it was considered that, despite their complexities, weight and size, tanks presented few mass production challenges that were not already within the capabilities of commercial car and truck production experience and practices to solve. One major company, Chrysler, went on to establish the Detroit Tank Arsenal, whilst the General Motors Corporation was also called upon to play a major role in tank production.

Part of the General Motors organisation was the Cadillac Motor Car Division, head-quartered in Detroit, Michigan. It considered that the major contribution it could make to the Light Tank engine supply situation was to utilise its existing production facilities to best effect. It accordingly proposed that its well-established commercial 5,700cc V-8 petrol engine could offer an alternative Light Tank engine installation. As each Cadillac car engine could produce 110hp, two of them could be coupled to provide sufficient power for the Light Tank series. It was further proposed that

Right:
Light Tank M5s
entering Tunis to
complete the first
US North African
campaign. As well as
the prominent white
star identification
markings it is
interesting to note
that white cross
markings have been
applied in the field to
reinforce the national
star markings. *(TM)*

the output could be further coupled to a Cadillac Hydra-Matic four-speed automatic transmission, also readily available from established Cadillac production facilities. Thanks to the war situation the prospects for civilian automobile sales were not promising yet the production facilities for engines and transmissions were established and capable of easing the light tank engine shortfalls.

During late 1941 a standard Light Tank M3 was converted to act as a test bed for the proposed Cadillac engine installation. It had the development vehicle designation of Light Tank M3E2. (The M3E1 was an Ordnance Department trials measure involving a Cummins diesel that did not prove successful.) Among the changes necessary to accommodate the two V-8 engines were a raised engine deck and a marginally longer superstructure to accommodate the bulk of the two engines. The raised deck became the prime recognition feature that differentiated the Light Tank M5 series from the M3 series. There were many internal changes, not the least being that the drive shaft location from the coupled engines to the transmission was in a much lower housing, making more working space available for the crew in the combat compartment as well as extra stowage space.

The conversion proved to be remarkably successful. As might have been expected, the well-tried engine and transmission caused no troubles at all. The driver's task was made much easier than before while the entire drive train ran smoothly. The success of the automotive installation was well demonstrated when the M3E2 prototype was driven under its own power from Detroit, Michigan, to the Aberdeen Proving Ground in Maryland, a distance of over 497 miles (800km), completely without troubles of any kind. This run, and many other trials, led to the Cadillac engine and transmission installation being approved, leading to type standardisation in February 1942. This was despite the lingering misgivings of some Ordnance Department officers who favoured the provision of air-cooled engines for tanks. Yet the aircraft engine supply situation had become so acute that their doubts had to be set aside and the Cadillac liquid-cooled engines were adopted, to be proven as trouble free.

Following the usual official procedures, after type standardisation it was initially decided that the Cadillac-engine model would

become the Light Tank M4. However, as the Medium Tank M4 was well established by early 1941 it was reconsidered that two tank types with the M4 designation could cause too many confusions. The Cadillac-built light tank therefore became the M5.

Production of the Light Tank M5 soon began at the Cadillac plant in Detroit, other manufacturers to be contracted later. Elsewhere, the transition from M3 to M5 production was virtually trouble-free as the welded hull of the latest M3 model, the M3A3,

complete with a sloping glacis plate, was carried over with only minor changes. Only the drive train was completely new.

There was one further modification to be introduced at a later stage, again carrying over a feature from the late production M3A3. This was the addition of a bulge at the rear of the turret to house the vehicle radio and some other items. Some other modifications were also introduced at this stage, such as improved, water-sealed hatches for the driver and co-driver, the provision of an escape hatch in the hull floor, and

some other constructional details. These changes were tested on another development vehicle, the M3E3, with approval soon forthcoming. Another sub-system tested on the M3E3 was a hydraulic drive for the turret. The changes resulted in the Light Tank M5A1, with type classification being approved on 24 September 1942. Production of the M5A1 commenced in November 1941 and by early 1943 all Light Tank series (M3 and M5) production lines had switched to the M5A1 model.

Although the M5 and M5A1 production

(cont page 16)

Above:
A Light Tank M5 configured for purely training purposes as no machine guns are installed. *(TM)*

Right:
Whenever possible all tank crews keep their vehicle armament covered to prevent dust and debris entering the barrels, as evident on this Light Tank M5. *(TM)*

Far right:
This US Army Light Tank M5A1 is seen during field exercises. The commander is in the process of throwing a smoke grenade to create a screen. *(TM)*

Left:
Light Tank M5A1s
operating in a
Pacific jungle during
late 1944 or early
1945. Note the lack
of the turret top
machine guns, no
doubt removed to
prevent damage
when operating
through dense
vegetation. *(TM)*

Above:
The Light Tank T7E1 built with a cast hull and turret armed with a 37mm main gun. This was the first in a series of vehicles intended to replace the existing M3/M5 series by eventually becoming the Medium Tank M7 armed with a 75mm gun. However, weights increased to the point where the M7 would have been seriously under-powered. In any event the M7 would only have supplemented the established Medium Tank M4 series so production was terminated after only 13 had been manufactured. *(TM)*

total had reached 8,884 by the time production ceased in June 1944, of these 6,810 were the M5A1. By 1944 the days of the M5 and M5A1 as viable combat vehicles were seen as almost over. Although both retained a useful combat role as reconnaissance vehicles they were of little use for anything other than low-intensity armoured warfare. By 1943 the 37mm main armament was inadequate and the armoured protection too light. Many of the combat roles once assigned to the Light Tank had therefore been assumed by the more capable Medium Tank M4 series, the Sherman. The Light Tank M5 was accordingly reclassified as Limited Standard during April 1943 after the M5A1 became available, and the M5A1 itself was reclassified as Substitute Standard in July 1944. Production of both had ceased when they were reclassified, but many served in one form or another until the war ended, gradually being supplemented from late 1944 onwards by the much more advanced and better-armed Light Tank M24, known in British service as the Chaffee. With the war over M5 and M5A1s were gradually retired from US Army service. An Ordnance listing dated October 1947 mentioned the M5A1 (but not the M5) as still

likely to be encountered in US Army service, although by then most must have been with the National Guard.

During the war years the M5/M5A1 featured prominently in the Lend-Lease Programme, the main recipients being the 'British Empire' (UK and Commonwealth forces), who received 1,391. The British Army knew both the M5 and M5A1 as the Stuart VI. The only other recipients were the Free French forces (413), and just five to the USSR (to add to the 1,676 of the M3 series models already supplied). One of the 'Soviet' M5A1s survives in a tank museum near Moscow, labelled as a M5A1 **СТЮАРТ** (Stuart).

From 1945 onwards, M5 and M5A1s retired from US Army service were distributed to various nations then considered as 'friendly' to US interests. Among them were Belgium, Bolivia, Brazil, Chile, the Dominican Republic, Ecuador, Guatemala, Haiti, Honduras, Indonesia, India, Mauritania, Mexico, South Korea, Paraguay, Taiwan, Uruguay and Venezuela. Some of these nations received M3 series vehicles as well as the M5/M5A1.

With these different nations the service careers of the last of the Light Tanks varied

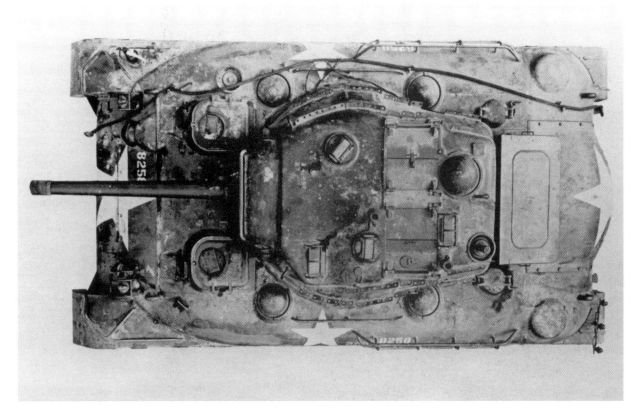

Some served only for brief periods - for instance the Belgian Army received ten M5A1s in 1948 and used them just for training the first post-war Belgian Army tank force until something better became available. With others their military usage was were far more prolonged. By the 1970s some nations had extended the useful service lives of their vehicles by the installation of suitable diesel engines but by the end of the 1970s numbers were beginning to diminish. Yet even in 2003 it was reported that the M3 and M5/M5A1 continued to remain in the defence inventory of Haiti, no doubt as a parades-only status symbol.

The replacement for the Light Tank M3 and M5 series was meant to be the Light Tank T7, but this never happened.

When it was first proposed during late 1941 the T7 was seen as an advanced design. Armed with a 37mm gun, the T7 had a cast hull and turret and was fitted with an air-cooled radial engine. Requests were then made for a 57mm gun and heavier armour, with the armament request finally being raised to a 75mm main gun. With all these extras the weight of the T7 raised the design out of the light tank category to the extent that the T7 was eventually type classified as the Medium Tank M7 in August 1942, with an initial order for 3,000 being placed.

By that time series production of the Medium Tank M4 was at maximum capacity and trials with the M7 pilot model revealed that the design was seriously overweight and thus under-powered. The Ordnance Department sensibly considered that fielding two medium tanks at the same time would create too much duplication of effort, especially as the long-term prospects for the M7 were unpromising. The production contract was therefore cancelled in February 1943 after only 13 had been produced by International Harvester at the specially commissioned and built Quad Cities Tank Arsenal at Bettendorf, Iowa. To add to the woeful tale of the M7, the Quad Cities production facility was then shut down in April 1943, soon after it had been completed, only to be reopened later as a tank overhaul centre.

In time, the US Army's M3/M5 series replacement emerged as the Light Tank M24, which did not enter front-line service until late 1944. The replacement process was far from complete when the war ended.

CHAPTER TWO

DESCRIPTION

The overall layout and form of the Light Tank M5 and
M5A1 was entirely conventional. It was also sturdy,
simple and easy to maintain. There were few changes from the
initial M5 model until M5A1 production was complete.

When considered in the usual light tank
terms, the Light Tank M5 and M5A1 were
large, almost as large as some
contemporary British cruiser tanks. The M5 series
had its design origin dating back to the 1930s, a
time when future armoured warfare requirements
were uncertain and future combat conditions still
unknown. In accordance with their usual
engineering approach to such matters, the
Americans therefore built big. As but one example
of this, the British Vickers Light Tank Mk V
weighed about 4.25 tons (4,320kg) and was armed
with two machine guns. Its close contemporary, the
US Light Tank M3 (from which the M5/M5A1
was later developed), weighed approximately 12.23
tons (12,430kg) and was armed with a 37mm gun
and three machine guns, a considerable disparity.

Apart from matters of scale, the M5/M5A1
light tanks were completely conventional. They
followed what was the usual US late 1930s tank
design and construction convention in that the
engine installation was at the rear, with drive
transmitted to a front-mounted transmission unit
and drive sprockets. Steering was by controlled
differentials.

Both the M5 and M5A1 had a crew of four:
commander and gunner in the turret fighting
compartment, the commander working as main
gun loader, with the driver and co-driver in the
hull front, seated either side of the transmission
unit. The co-driver, who was also provided with a
set of driving controls, doubled as the hull
machine gunner. He also contributed to the crew
mainly in being an extra body for the routine
day-to-day driving, sentry, maintenance and
domestic tasks which would otherwise have been
more burdensome when shared by a crew of just
three.

Within the turret the commander and
gunner were provided with seats which were
adjustable both horizontally and vertically - these
could be locked in any position. The seats were
secured to the turret basket enabling them to
rotate with the turret, a feature not present on
some of the earlier Light Tank series.

Each member of the crew had his own access
or escape hatch. On the M5A1 these hatches
were enlarged and extra attention was made
regarding sealing against water ingress. Also on
the M5A1, an additional escape hatch was
provided in the hull floor. Whenever possible, the
driver and co-driver operated with their
access hatches open for head-up vision by
raising their seats.

Above:
The first Light Tank M5A1 photographed during trials at the Rock Island Arsenal, Maryland, USA. *(TM)*

Left:
The British Army named the Light Tank M5 and M5A1 as the Stuart VI. This example, an M5A1, was one of the very first to arrive in Britain under the Lend-Lease programme during 1942. *(TM)*

Above:
Items to note on this Rock Island Arsenal photograph of the first Light Tank M5A1 are the intended tool stowage positions (not always followed in the field) and the rubber track shoes. Note also the lack of the turret machine gun. *(TM)*

Right:
Rear view of one of the first Stuart VI tanks (Light Tank M5A1) delivered to the British Army. Once in service, vehicles were rarely maintained in such a pristine condition. *(TM)*

For the M5, vision devices for the crew when closed down consisted of three M6 periscopes held in traversing turntable-type mountings. Two of these protruded through the front superstructure hatches, for the driver and co-driver. The other periscope was for the commander, mounted in the turret roof. On the M5A1 the commander's periscope mounting was provided with a full 360° traverse, with another M6 periscope added to provide vision to the rear of the turret. A direction finder fastened to the turret just ahead of the commander's periscope indicated the straight ahead position at all times. Another accessory for the commander was a turret roof-mounted spotlight.

As with the earlier Light Tank M3 series, there were three M5/M5A1 main assemblies to be manufactured: hull, superstructure and turret. The hull and superstructure relied on a strong form of monocoque construction, being assembled from flat sheets of face-hardened, homogeneous rolled armour steel plate and seam welded. At the time the US light tanks were designed, the advantages of sloped or smooth-contoured cast armour were yet to be discovered. The only sloping surface of any note on the M5 and M5A1 was the one-

piece sloping glacis plate that not only provided better forward protection but also added to the available internal space - it was also less time consuming to produce than the earlier windshield-type front superstructure. On the M5A1 further stowage space was available following the provision of an optional stowage box on the hull rear.

By the time the M5 entered production, earlier problems regarding US tank armour availability had been overcome by several measures. Not the least of these was the diversion of several steel manufacturing concerns towards the production of face-hardened plates, a process that few had ever been involved with before. The most important supplier of armour for the M5 series became the American Car & Foundry Company of Berwick, Pennsylvania, although there were other suppliers. In addition to its armour production, the American Car & Foundry Co was involved in US light tank production from almost the beginning during 1939 (from the Light Tank M2A4 onwards) until 1944, when it completed its last M5A1.

In general terms M5 series construction closely followed that of the earlier M3 series although with thicker armour on the hull and superstructure - turret armour thicknesses

Above:
Items to note on this overhead view of a late production Light Tank M5A1 are the covers for the turret machine gun, the track grousers (spuds) stowed around the turret and the addition of an equipment stowage box on the hull rear. *(TM)*

Above:
Light Tank M5 vehicle maintenance in the field during the European winter of 1944/45. The crew are applying white paint for camouflage purposes. *(TM)*

remained virtually unchanged. The actual thicknesses were as follows:

Hull front, upper	2.5in (63.5mm)
Hull front, lower	2 to 2.5in (50.8 to 63.5mm)
Sides and rear	1 to 1.13in (25.4 to 28.6mm)
Top	.5in (12.7mm)
Bottom	.37 to .5in (9.5 to 12.7mm)
Turret, front	2in (50.8mm)
Turret, sides and rear	1.25in (31.8mm)
Turret top	.5in (12.7mm)

As early as 1941, this armoured protection was inadequate against virtually all contemporary anti-tank weapons, but did provide overall protection for the crew against small arms fire and artillery shell splinters.

The turret was formed around a curved all-welded homogeneous armour plate, the main difference between the M5 and M5A1 being that on the M5A1 the rear of the turret formed an integral bulge in which the main radio installation was housed. This increased the available space in the fighting compartment, separated from the engine compartment by a steel bulkhead. The M5A1 turret had a removable plate in the rear of the bulge through which the 37mm main gun could be removed for replacement or repair. The turret ring diameter was 3.89ft (1.187m) making space inside the turret very limited.

Turret drive on the M5 series was hydraulic, the turret rotating on three main roller bearing assemblies. On the M5A1 the commander was provided with an auxiliary manual drive to rotate the turret. Three pistol ports were provided in the turret sides, each with a Protectoscope for vision purposes. On the M5A1 the ports were deleted, their places being covered by small lockable hatches.

The engine compartment housed the two 5,700cc V-8 Cadillac Series 42 side-valve liquid-cooled petrol engines coupled together, the engine installation being the main feature that differentiated the Light Tank M5 series from previous light tanks. They were originally designed (and used) as car engines, with each V-cylinder bank set at angle of 90° from the other.

The engines were coupled to the transfer box at the flywheel end of each engine. Each engine could provide 110hp at 3,400rpm (the available power being a reflection of contemporary US commercial automobile design and the low cost of petrol [gasoline] in the US), so the combined output of the two engines was 220hp. The maximum governed speed of each engine was 4,000rpm.

This power output was sufficient to allow a theoretical road speed of 36mph (58km/h), although actual speeds were usually kept lower. Cooling air was drawn through louvres in the top of the engine deck behind the turret ring, to be passed through the two radiators and oil coolers located over the engines, with belt-driven radiator cooling fans drawing the air

(cont page 29)

Above:
The crew of this Light Tank M5 appear to be from the Greek army. The corner-hinged hull access hatches indicate that this is an M5 and shows how turret traverse was limited when these were raised. *(TM)*

Right:
Right-hand view of the V-8 Cadillac Series 42 engine, two of which powered the Light Tank M5 series. They were originally well-proven commercial petrol engines that proved to be highly dependable in the military role. The elongated unit to the left of the main engine unit is the automatic gearbox.

Below:
The controlled differential and transfer box unit as fitted on the Light Tank M5/M5A1 series. This unit was located immediately behind and below the front hull (glacis) plate. Note the couplings for the individual drive shafts from each engine/gearbox unit.

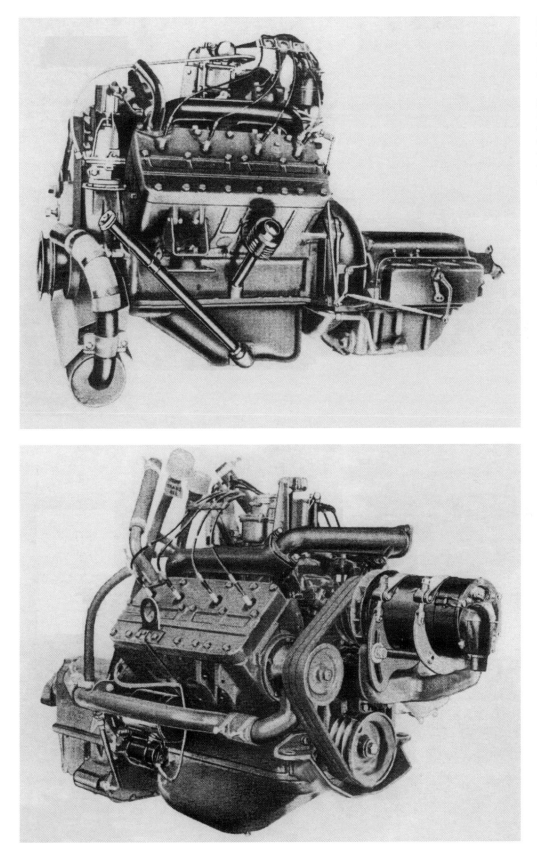

Left:
Left-hand side of the V-8 Cadillac Series 42. Each engine was capable of producing 110hp. The automatic gearbox unit on the right of the main engine assembly connected to the transfer box at the front of the vehicle via a short propeller shaft.

Left:
Right-hand rear view of the V-8 Cadillac Series 42 petrol engine showing one cylinder bank and the coolant pipes that connected the engine to the overhead radiator assembly for cooling. The prominent assembly driven by the fan belt is a combined water pump and electric-power generator.

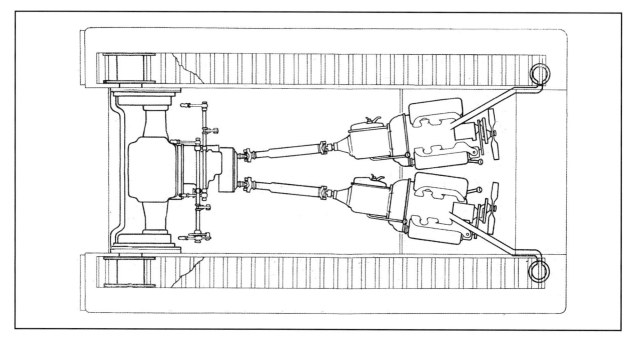

Above:
A diagram of the engine and drive train installation on the Light Tank M5/M5A1. Note how the two engines are mounted pointing inwards and linked to the steering unit at the front of the tank.

Right:
Each Light Tank M5/M5A1 was fitted with a small auxiliary generator unit for battery charging and to provide basic power when the main engines were switched off. The unit was fitted under the floor of the main compartment.

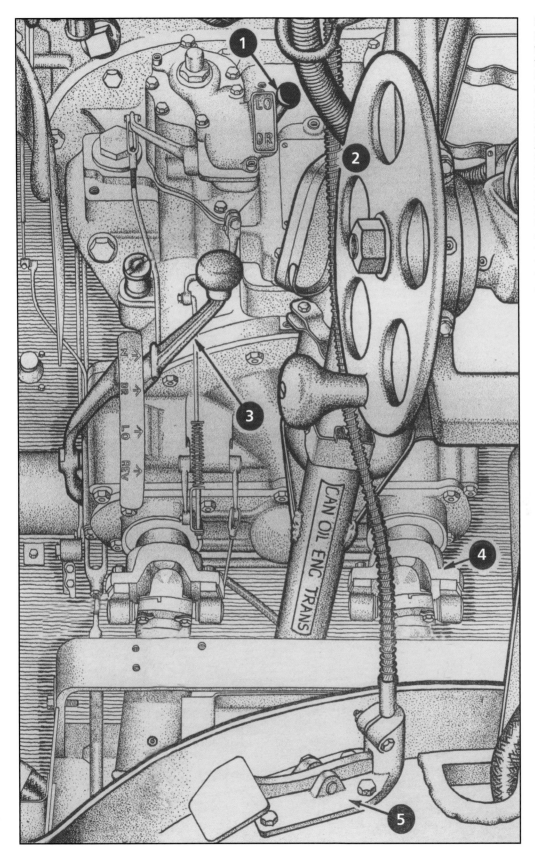

Left:
Looking forward from the gunner's position towards the driver. Item 5 at the bottom of the drawing is the main gun firing pedal. Item 4 is one of the two universal coupling joints for the propeller shafts connected to the transfer box. Item 3 is the gear selector lever while the prominent Item 2 is the gunner's barrel elevating control wheel. Item 1 is the transmission forward/reverse control.

Above:
Field repairs for the
steering and transfer
box unit on a Light
Tank M5, the entire
front plate having
been removed for
access to the unit or
for removal and
replacement. *(TM)*

Right:
The early pattern
driver's instrument
panel for a Light Tank
M5 or M5A1. Note
that most of the
instruments and
control buttons are
duplicated to cater
for the twin engine
installation. In the
lower centre is
the speedometer
calibrated up to
an 'optimistic'
80mph. *(TM)*

down into the engine area. It was the location and space needed for the radiators that made necessary the raised rear deck of the M5 series. Radiator refilling access covers were set into the top decking.

Engine access through the engine covers for repairs and maintenance was considered to be generally good, while a complete power pack replacement involved few problems and could be completed relatively rapidly.

Engine fuel, 70 or 80 octane petrol, was carried in two main tanks, one in each of the sponsons located along the superstructure, each side of the engine compartment. Each tank had a single refilling access cover, with drain plugs under the hull. Total fuel capacity was 74gals (337ltr), sufficient for a cruising range of approximately 99 miles (160km). No provision was made on the M5 series for the two jettisonable auxiliary tanks supplied as an option on the M3 series, as it appears the facility was rarely used, being vulnerable to incoming fire. Even so, fuel jerricans were frequently slung along each side of the hull when on operations.

Drive from each engine to the transmission unit at the front was through a propeller shaft under the combat compartment floor. This proved a great advantage to the turret occupants, as on the M3 series, with radial engines, the propeller shaft had to be routed from the central point of the engine, high in the engine compartment. The shaft housing was therefore angled downwards through the M3's combat compartment, occupying so much internal space that it could create problems when traversing the turret. By routeing the propeller shaft under the floor on the M5/M5A1 a significant amount of working and stowage space was freed for better use, including, for instance, extra ammunition stowage.

Propeller shafts connected the engine output to a transfer unit mounted centrally under the glacis plate. The heart of the drive unit was the Cadillac Hydra-Matic (sometimes written as Hydramatic) automatic gearbox, another mechanical unit taken from existing Cadillac commercial production lines. The

Above:
This Light Tank M5A1 has extra frontal protection made-up by simply adding lengths of logs. This was to provide extra stand-off protection against close range *Panzerfaust* or *Raketenpanzerbüchse* shaped-charge warheads. The location is Germany in the winter of 1944/45. *(TM)*

Above:
The caption for this heavily retouched photograph of a Light Tank M5A1 is 'Mail from Home'. The censor did not see fit to remove detail such as the tarpaulin stowage at the rear of the hull or the presence of an extra stowage box behind the turret bustle. *(TM)*

gearbox units, plus a two-speed reduction gearbox in the transfer case, provided six forward speeds and one reverse. The driver (or co-driver) controlled the transmission unit in exactly the same way as on a civilian automobile by simply selecting forward, reverse or neutral by operating the gear selector lever. The gearboxes automatically selected the appropriate gear according to the degree of accelerator pedal depression, thereby considerably reducing the driver's workload.

The final drive was taken through a short shaft each side of the transmission unit to the final drive sprockets. Each herringbone-type sprocket had 13 teeth, driving tracks with 66, type T16 rubber block track shoes double-pinned together on each side. Each track shoe was 11.6in (295mm) wide. Lengths of spare track were frequently carried slung across the front of the vehicle for extra protection. Forged steel grousers (or spuds) could be added, one to every sixth shoe, to improve traction when required. When not in use the grousers were carried on brackets fitted to the sides of the turret. The tracks were tensioned by adjustment of the idler wheel at the

rear. Three track support rollers were provided each side. By the time the M5A1 appeared detachable sand shields over the tracks were a standard fixture but were often removed to ease maintenance access to the suspension units and tracks, or to prevent mud and debris clogging them under wet conditions.

As mentioned earlier in this chapter, steering was via controlled differentials. These provided a minimum turning radius of 21ft (6.4m).

On both the M5 and M5A1 the suspension was of the same pattern as that used for other US light tanks and early production series medium tanks of the period. Light tanks had two suspension units each side, with three on medium tanks. All were of the Vertical Volute Suspension System (VVSS) type, that proved durable and easy to maintain while providing a reasonably smooth ride for the vehicle occupants. If any damage occurred, each unit could be easily unbolted and replaced, while they did not impinge on internal space. Each suspension unit carried two rubber-tyred 20 x 6in road wheels with a spoke pattern. There were four road wheels each track.

Above:
Late production Light Tank M5A1s had several features not installed on earlier models. Seen here are the sand shields over the tracks and the curved armoured fairing intended to protect the turret machine gun mounting. *(TM)*

Left:
The same vehicle as above showing the added equipment stowage box over the hull rear, and the revised grouser (spuds) stowage on the left-hand side of the turret made necessary by the addition of the curved shield for the turret machine gun mounting. *(TM)*

Specifications

Model	M5	M5A1
Crew	Four (commander, driver, co-driver, gunner)	
Weight	14.73 tons (14,970kg)	15.14 tons (15,380kg)
Length	14.20ft (4.33m)	15.88ft (4.839m*)
Width	7.35ft (2.24m)	7.87ft (2.4m**)
Height	7.55ft (2.3m)	7.55ft (2.3m)
Track	6.13ft (1.87m)	6.13ft (1.87m)
Track width	11.6in (295mm)	11.6in (295mm)
Length of track on ground	9.74ft (2.97m)	9.74ft (2.97m)
Ground clearance	1.15ft (349mm)	1.15ft (349mm)
Max speed, road	36mph (58km/h)	36mph (58km/h)
Fuel capacity	74gals (337ltr)	74gals (337ltr)
Range, road, cruising	99 miles (160km)	99 miles (160km)
Fording	3ft (914mm)	3ft (914mm)
Vertical obstacle	1.5ft (457mm)	1.5ft (457mm)

Left:
A US Army Light
Tank M5 leading an
array of Allied armour
out of the Normandy
beachhead, probably
during July 1944. *(TM)*

The bottom of the combat compartment also housed a single-cylinder, petrol-driven auxiliary power unit provided to supplement the engine-driven generators for battery charging. If required, this auxiliary unit could also power the radios and intercom when the main engines were not running. Both the M5 and M5A1 had a 12V electric system, with a 50A generator, driven from the main engine, supplying a single 12V battery.

Part of the electrical system powered the main radio equipment. This could be one of three types: SCR-508 (for tank forces), SCR-528 (within mechanised formations) or the general issue SCR-538. Command tanks carried an extra set, the SCR-506, that could automatically transmit in code form. On British Stuart VI tanks the main radio installation was a No 19. All these equipments used whip antennae. To communicate via semaphore signals under radio silence conditions, each vehicle also carried a Flag Set M238. For internal communications each crew member was provided with an interphone (intercom) station, a headset and a microphone.

Among the standard equipment carried on each vehicle was a recovery/towing cable, two towing shackles being fitted at each end of the hull. Other standard equipment included a fixed fire extinguisher in the engine compartment, plus a smaller, hand-held portable type in the combat compartment. Another equipment, not always carried, was a Decontaminating Apparatus M2 in case of chemical agent attack. Various track maintenance and pioneer tools were carried over the hull rear.

Trench crossing width	5.33ft (1.625m)	5.33ft (1.625m)
Gradient	60%	60%
Engine installation	Two 5,700cc V-8 Cadillac Series 42 side-valve liquid-cooled petrol engines, each developing 110hp at 3,400rpm	
Transmission	Cadillac Hydra-Matic automatic with four forward and one reverse gears	
Steering	controlled differential	controlled differential
Turning radius	21ft (6.4m)	21ft (6.4m)
Suspension	VVSS	VVSS
Electrical system	12V	12V
Armour	see text	see text
Armament	One 37mm Gun M6	
	Two 0.30-calibre Machine Guns M1919A4	
	One 0.30-calibre Machine Gun M1919A5	
	One 0.45-calibre sub-machine gun	

* over stowage box, otherwise as M5   ** over sand shields

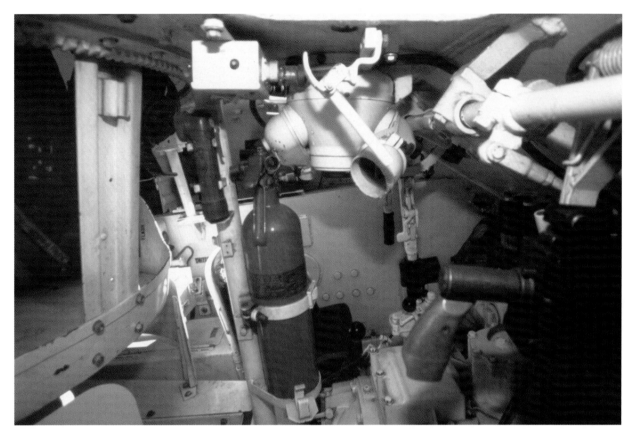

Above:
A view from the co-driver's seat looking towards the driver's position. Items to note are the side of the turret basket on the left, the fire extinguisher between the driver and co-driver, and the pistol grip for the 0.30-calibre M1919A4 flexible-mounted hull machine gun in the right foreground. *(JBn)*

Right:
A service manual sketch indicating the standard equipment stowage positions around the driver's position in the Stuart VI. Needless to say, not all equipment was stowed to these guidelines once in the field.

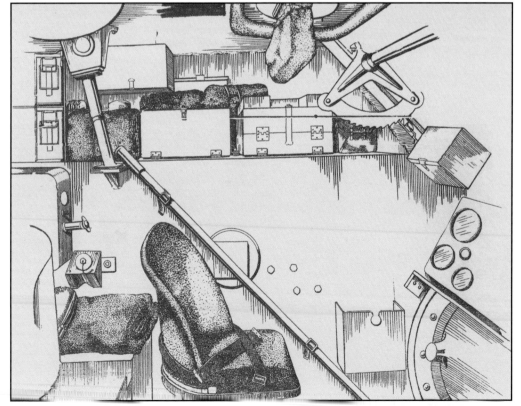

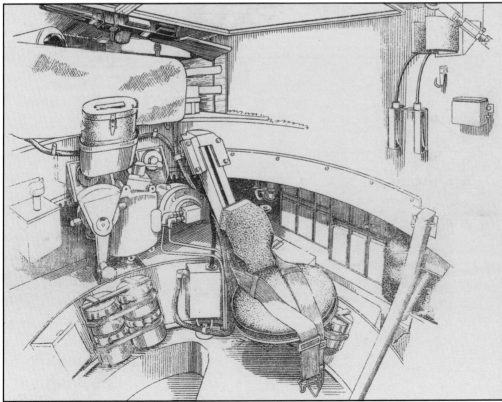

Above:
Looking down through the driver's access hatch, showing his seat at the bottom of the picture. Also visible are the gear selector lever and the relative bulk of the transfer box and steering unit. The right-hand steering lever is visible in the top left corner. *(JBn)*

Left:
Not normally seen so clearly is the gunner's area and seat on a Stuart VI. This is a service manual illustration of ideal stowage positions - not always easily followed in combat.

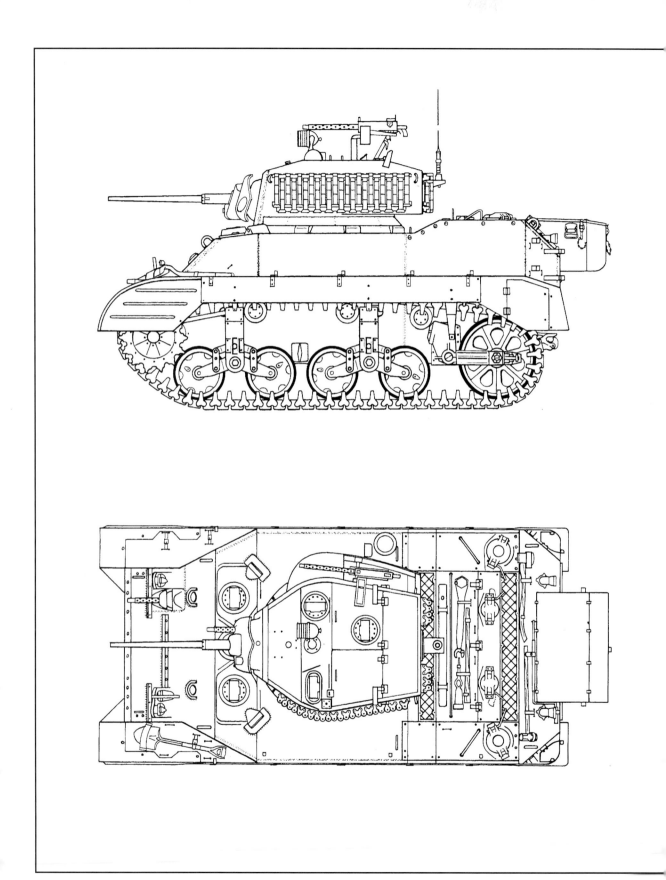

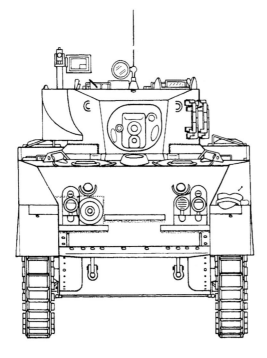

M5A1 Late
(Scale 1:35)

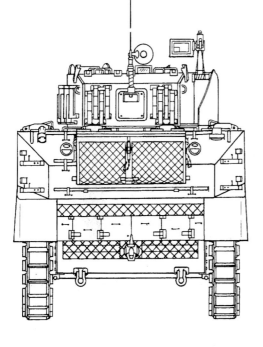

© 2004 DP. Dyer.

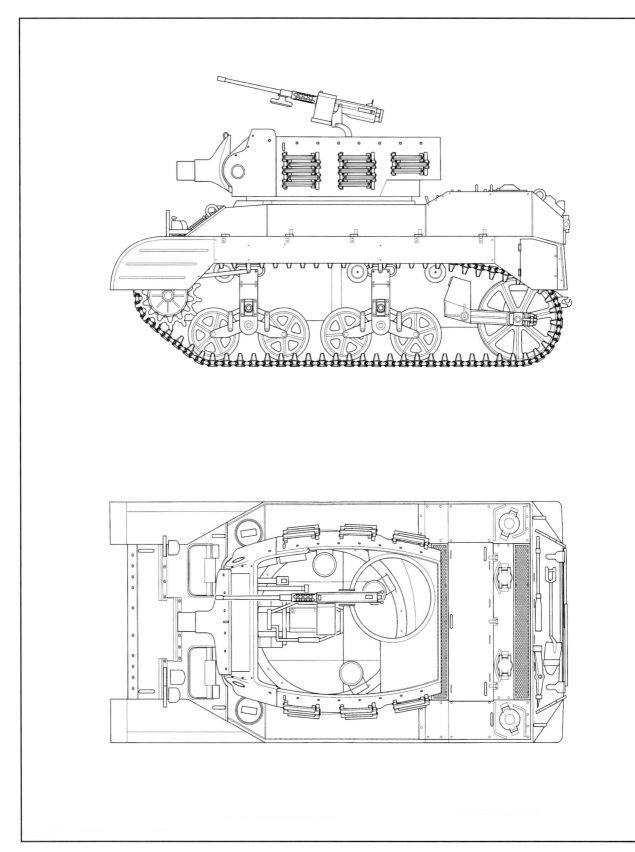

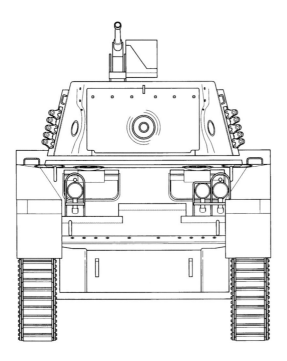

M8 Howitzer Motor Carriage
(Scale 1:35)

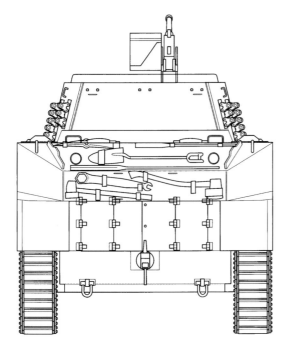

CHAPTER THREE

ARMAMENT

Both the Light Tank M5 and M5A1 were fitted with the 37mm Gun M6 throughout production. The M8 Howitzer Motor Carriage carried a 75mm Howitzer M1A1. Despite the limitations of their main armament, both had involved development histories.

The main armament of the Light Tank M5 and M5A1 was the 37mm Gun M6, which originally started life as a towed anti-tank gun for the Infantry. Development of the towed gun began during 1937 when the US Army realised that to keep pace with developments elsewhere it would need some form of anti-armour weapon but had nothing in its inventory. A rapid survey of the international anti-tank gun market followed to gain some idea of what might be needed, resulting in the purchase of two 3.7cm PaK 35/36 guns from Rheinmetall-Borsig of Germany for testing.

37mm Gun M6

After studying these two guns the designers at the Ordnance Department, Rock Island and Watervliet Arsenals, produced two tentative designs before deciding that these efforts would result in nothing better than the German original so that was utilised as the basis for the US Army's production model, the 37mm Gun M3 on Carriage M4. The designers were in good company as the Rheinmetall-Borsig design was also adopted by Japan and the Soviet Union as well as the Germans.

The 37mm Gun M3 differed in several respects from the German original, the most noticeable exterior difference being the rounded curves and contours of the US-designed breech ring. The latter refinement was to prove something of an unnecessary complication since the German design was much easier to mass produce, requiring far less machining. However, this was overlooked at the time of the M3's type classification and the same gun was adopted as a tank gun, the only changes from the towed gun being the mounting and the few alterations necessary to make the gun fit into a turret mounting. Both the towed and tank guns were ballistically identical and fired the same fixed ammunition.

The initial tank gun model was the 37mm Gun M5, developed during the late 1930s and ordered into production during the summer of 1940. With the anticipated manufacturing facility, Watervliet Arsenal, already very busy it was decided to share the production task with US general industry, initially with the unlikely sounding United Shoe Machinery Company and the National Pneumatic Company.

The two companies found the Gun M5 relatively straightforward to produce so by early

(cont page 44)

Above:
The precarious position that a commander might have to be in when using the turret machine gun, particularly when the hull access hatches were open. In fact this is a posed photograph as the canvas cartridge belt is empty. *(TM)*

Left:
The turret roof of a Light Tank M5A1 shows the gunner's roof sight visor and the commander's two rotating periscopic vision devices. Also visible are the periscopic vision devices for the driver and co-driver. The turret machine gun is not installed although its mounting is protected by a canvas cover. *(TM)*

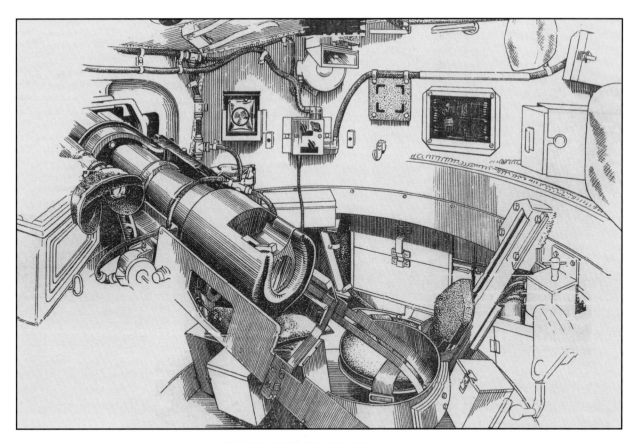

Above:
The interior of an M5 from the gunner's position, although this service manual illustration gives an unrealistic perspective. Note how the breech of the 37mm Gun M6 dominates the turret interior and the position of the commander's seat. *(TM)*

Right:
Looking down through the gunner's access hatch and into the turret basket. The gunner's seat is prominent, as is the breech of the 37mm Gun M6. Main gun ammunition stowage can be seen beneath and to the right of the breech. *(JDn)*

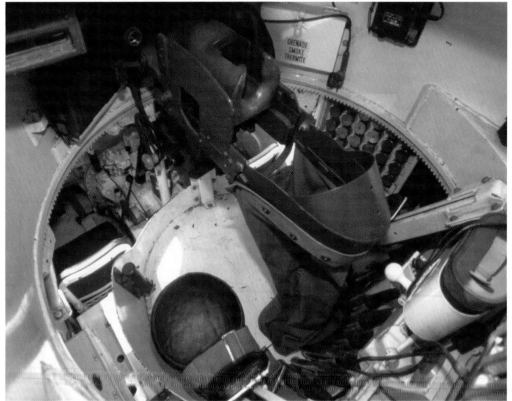

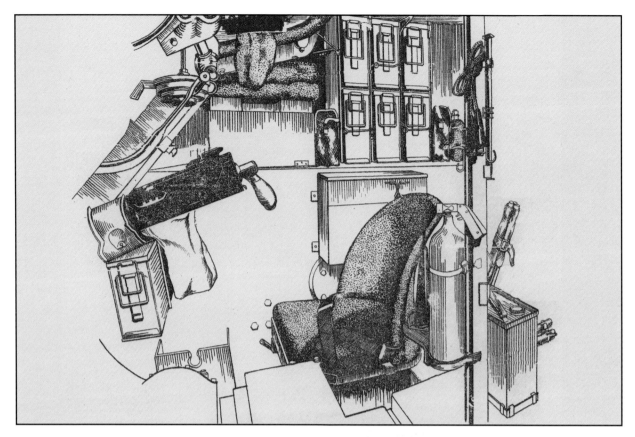

Above:
Looking from the driver's position towards the co-driver's location with the breech mechanism of the hull machine gun in front of the seat. Ammunition boxes for machine gun are located to the right and just above the seat.

Left:
The mounting for the 37mm Gun M6 on a Light Tank M5A1. The breech mechanism was semi-automatic in that the vertical sliding breech block opened to eject the used cartridge case when the gun was at its full recoil length. Note the canvas bag, attached to the recoil bars, to catch spent shell cases. *(JBn)*

Above:
The towed 37mm Gun M3 on Carriage M4 from which the 37mm Gun M6 tank gun was developed. In fact the gun in the foreground is an M3A1 as it is fitted with a multi-baffle muzzle brake which was not only difficult to manufacture but was really unnecessary as the towed carriage could readily absorb all firing stresses. The muzzle brake was therefore omitted for series production. *(TG)*

December 1941 a total of 2,800 guns had been completed. During that same month a slightly modified model, the 37mm Gun M6, became the standard and was the only model produced from then onwards. In fact the M5 and M6 guns were inter-changeable, worn M5 barrel tubes being replaced by M6 tubes. By late 1941 the M6 was already in production with American Tyre Founders who had manufactured about 900 by the end of 1941. At that time a total requirement for over 35,000 guns was foreseen, including a number for the British. By the time 37mm Gun M6 production ceased during 1944 that total had been exceeded by a significant margin.

By December 1941 the total of 37mm tank guns manufactured was 5,571. The actual annual production totals were as follows:

1940	1941	1942	1943	1944
491	5,080	23,839	13,825	4,000
Total	47,235			

Not all these guns were allocated to the Light Tank series. Several other vehicles, including wheeled tank destroyers, armoured cars and reconnaissance cars, also mounted the 37mm

Gun M6. The gun also featured in the Lend-Lease Programme.

The gun itself, 53.5 calibres long, was entirely conventional, being largely constructed from high-grade steel. The breech operation was semi-automatic, the vertical sliding wedge-type breech block opening at the end of the recoil cycle to eject the empty case and cocking the firing mechanism at the same time. Recoil was controlled by a heavy oil, hydrospring mechanism under the barrel, the usual recoil length being 7in (178mm). It was fired by a solenoid connected to a trigger, although a mechanical trigger mechanism (operated by a foot pedal) was also available. In theory it was possible to fire up to 20 rounds a minute by a trained crew, the commander acting as loader. The total weight of the gun and its breech mechanism was 190lb (86.2kg).

On the Light Tank M5 the M6 gun was mounted with a co-axial 0.30-calibre Machine Gun M1919A5 in a Combination Mount M23. On the M5A1 the same gun and machine gun were combined in a Combination Mount M44. The change of mounting was introduced to realign the angle of the optical sights' eyepieces, enabling the gunner to use the sights more

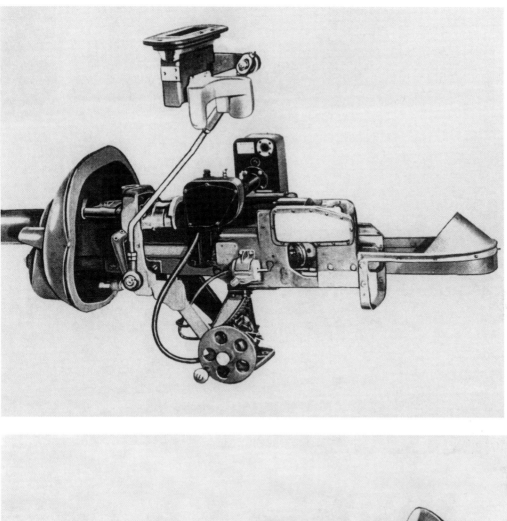

Left:
Left-hand view of the Combination Gun Mount M23 or M44, the only difference between the two being the mounting angle of the optical sights, the M44 allowing easier firing at high elevation angles. The inter-connecting rod between the mounting trunnion and sight unit can be seen.

Below:
Right-hand view of the Combination Gun Mount M23 or M44. As a general rule the Mount M23 was installed on the Light Tank M5 and the Mount M44 on the Light Tank M5A1. The position of the M1919A5 co-axial machine gun can be seen.

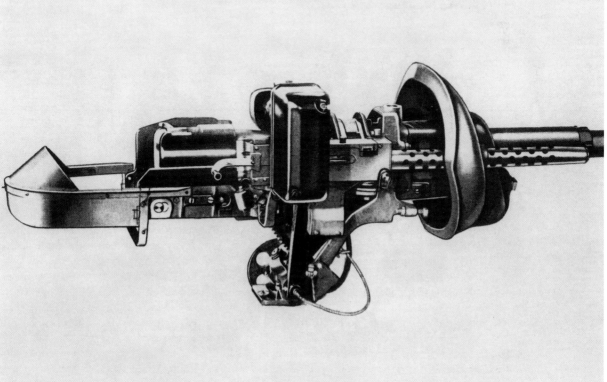

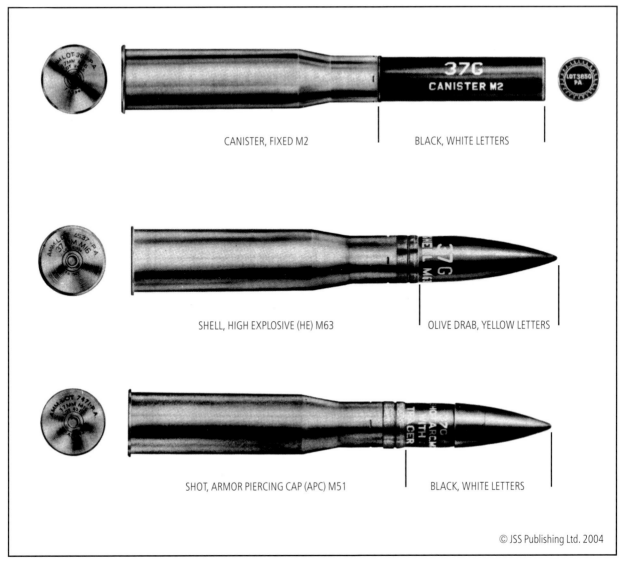

CANISTER, FIXED M2

BLACK, WHITE LETTERS

SHELL, HIGH EXPLOSIVE (HE) M63

OLIVE DRAB, YELLOW LETTERS

SHOT, ARMOR PIERCING CAP (APC) M51

BLACK, WHITE LETTERS

© JSS Publishing Ltd. 2004

easily at higher angles of elevation without the physical contortions needed when using the M23 mount. Both mounts fixed the gun in a cast steel shield (mantlet) that protected almost the entire front face of the turret, the outlines of the M44 being more angular than for the M23.

The gun traversed through a full 360° with the turret, barrel elevation and depression angles being +20° and -10° respectively. Elevation changes were made by turning a hand wheel. The gun mounting was auto-stabilised in elevation under gyroscopic control, by a hydraulic powered system. This allowed the gun to be aimed and fired with an improved expectation of a hit which the vehicle was moving. On the M5 the main stabiliser pump

and power units were located just under the turret ring. The extra space available in the M5A1 turret interior allowed these units to be relocated to the combat compartment floor.

The gunner had two optical systems for aiming and fire control. One was the Telescope M70D, a x3 magnification instrument with a field of view of just over 12°. The sight graticule was calibrated up to 4,800ft (1,463m). An alternative system, normally used for target acquisition rather than gun aiming, was a Periscope M4A1 combined with a Telescope M40A2, the latter having a x1.44 magnification and a field of view of 9°. The main drawback of the 37mm Gun M6 was that it became obsolete almost as soon as it entered service but it was effective for the role selected for the Light Tank M5 and M5A1.

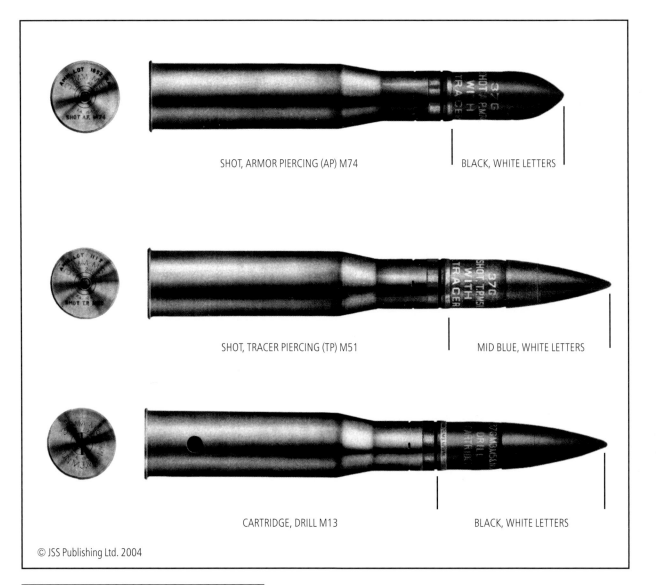

SHOT, ARMOR PIERCING (AP) M74   BLACK, WHITE LETTERS

SHOT, TRACER PIERCING (TP) M51   MID BLUE, WHITE LETTERS

CARTRIDGE, DRILL M13   BLACK, WHITE LETTERS

37mm Ammunition

The ammunition for the M6 tank gun was the same as that for the towed M3 gun but with one additional development that was only rarely fired from the towed gun. The four standard operational rounds by 1944 were as follows:

Shell, High Explosive M63 (HE)
Shot, Armor Piercing M74 (AP)
Shot, Armor Piercing Cap M51 (APC)
Canister, Fixed M2

All these rounds were fixed, ie the projectile and propellant case were issued, handled and loaded in one piece. The cartridge cases, each 8.75in (222mm) long and with a percussion primer in the centre of the base, were brass (M16) or steel (M16B1), containing varying weights of propellant. For logistic and production planning purposes the propellant weight was a nominal .5lb (227g). The actual propellant weights for each round are given below.

The Shell, High Explosive M63 (HE) was used as a directly fired general purpose round against unarmoured targets. It was not very effective as the 1.61lb (730g) projectile had a TNT payload weighing only .085lb (38.5g) so the resultant shell body fragmentation radius was limited. The payload was ignited on impact with a target by a M58 base fuse. The propellant weight was .44lb (198.5g), sufficient to provide a muzzle velocity of 2,651ft/s (808m/s). The projectile was painted olive green.

The Shot, Armor Piercing M74 (AP) projectile

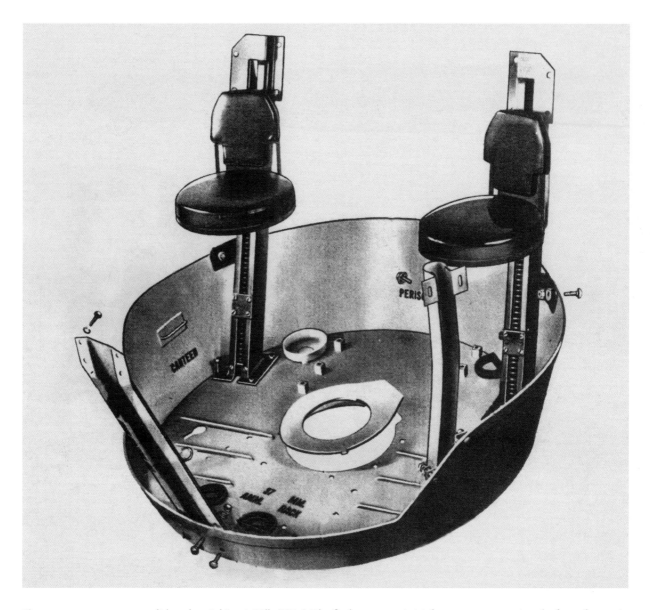

Above:
The turret basket
for the Light Tank
M5/M5A1 showing
the positions for the
adjustable height
seats, the gunner
being on the right in
this illustration and
the commander on
the left.

was solid steel, weighing 1.92lb (871g). The flat base of the projectile contained a tracer element that burned for three seconds to provide a visual indication of the trajectory but that was all – there was no explosive filling. The blunt nose penetrator was concealed under an aerodynamically shaped nose cone to reduce drag until it struck the target. Official armour penetration figures state that this round could penetrate 1.42in (36mm) of armour at 1,500ft (457m). The cartridge case contained .51lb (229.6g) of propellant, imparting a muzzle velocity of 2,598ft/s (792m/s). The projectile was painted black.

The Shot, Armor Piercing Cap M51 (APC) had a ballistic cap, once again behind an aerodynamically shaped nose cone, the cap imparting

an initial target penetration before the main solid steel penetrator mass provided the penetration of 2.4in (61mm) of armour at 1,500ft (457m). Once again there was no explosive payload, the flat base of the projectile housing a tracer element that burned for three seconds. Two types of APC M51 round were produced. The M51B1 had a pointed ballistic cap; for the M51B2 this was rounded. Part of the APC M51's improved armour penetration performance compared to the AP M74 projectile was due to a slight increase in propellant load to .53lb (241g), imparting a muzzle velocity of 2,900ft/s (884m/s). The projectile was painted black and weighed 1.92lb (871g).

The special-to-type round for the M6 tank gun

was the Canister Fixed M2, an anti-personnel round used to neutralise nearby enemy infantry. It could also be used to clear vegetation to expose a possible target. The projectile was a thin-walled tin canister that broke up almost immediately after it left the muzzle. Packed inside the blunt-nosed canister were 122 steel balls, each .37in (9.5mm) in diameter, held in a resin matrix. As the canister broke open the steel balls travelled towards the target in a pattern at an initial velocity of 2,500ft/s (762m/s). The balls spread out in the same manner as for a shotgun blast, but soon lost their energy to the extent that the maximum effective range was, at best, 748ft (228m). The canister weighed 1.94lb (880g) and was painted black. The propellant charge weighed .52lb (234g).

On the M5 the 37mm ammunition stowage capacity was 123 rounds. On the M5A1 this was increased to 147 rounds.

For training the Shot, Tracer Practice M51 (TP) was available. The relatively low-cost mild steel projectile was intended to replicate the ballistic characteristics of the APC M51. It contained a tracer element in the flat base.

For really low-cost gun loading training in barrack areas or on restricted outdoor ranges there was the Rifle, Subcaliber, 0.22 M5. This was a short 0.22-calibre rifle barrel held inside what resembled a one-piece, blunt-nosed 37mm cartridge formed from a bronze casting. With a 0.22 round inserted, the entire assembly was loaded into the gun breech in the usual fashion and, after aiming, it was fired following normal drill procedures. The base of the 0.22 cartridge could be struck by the usual firing pin in the gun's breech block so that, as it fired, a mechanical device operated the usual case extractors so that the breech opened in the usual manner. The device could then be reloaded with a fresh cartridge and reused.

75mm Howitzer M1A1

The 75mm howitzer that formed the main armament of the M8 Howitzer Motor Carriage (HMC) was originally designed during the 1920s as a Pack Howitzer to be carried by a team of six mules. The howitzer, type classified in 1927 as the 75mm Howitzer M1 on Carriage M1, could therefore be assembled from six sub-assemblies. A redesign of the breech block and the associated breech ring later resulted in the M1A1. When it

was decided to adapt the M1A1 howitzer for mounting in the M8 turret some redesign work had to be made to the usual barrel support surround, resulting in a new type classification of 75mm Howitzer M2.

The original intention was that howitzers to arm the M8 HMC vehicles would be obtained by modifying existing M1A1 barrels but that source of supply was soon exhausted, especially at a time when the same barrels were in great demand for the 75mm Pack Howitzer M8 (Airborne). More barrels therefore had to be manufactured from new. It was then possible to make the barrel support as an integral part of the weapon resulting in a new type classification, the 75mm Howitzer M3.

In practice the M2 and M3 howitzers were inter-changeable by way of the one mounting type necessary for the M8 HMC turret. This was the Mount M7, with barrel elevation limits of –20° to +40°, the barrel traversing through a full 360° with the turret. Spring equilibriators were provided to balance the weight of the breech and its mechanism on the gun-mounting trunnion bearings.

The M2 and M3 both had the same horizontal sliding-type breech block mechanism secured to a short barrel just 15.93 calibres long. Recoil was controlled by heavy oil, hydrospring dampers under the barrel, the usual recoil length being 11.6in (295mm). Firing was carried out using an electrical solenoid operated trigger, although a mechanical trigger mechanism operated by a lanyard formed an alternative. A trained crew could fire six rounds a minute for short periods, the normal fire rate being three rounds per minute. Total weight of the howitzer and its breech mechanism was 341lb (154.7kg).

As the howitzer was an indirect fire weapon the gun layer was provided with the usual complement of indirect fire instruments. One of these was the Telescope, Panoramic, M12A5, a special-to-type adaptation of the standard US artillery dial sight, with graticules to allow the howitzer to be aimed for direct fire at ranges up to 1,600yd (1,463m) in an emergency. For this role the fully traversable sight head had to be pointing on the same line as the barrel. Normally the dial sight would be used by placing the standard graticule against a fixed point at any location around the vehicle to permit controlled traverse corrections to be made as fire was corrected by a forward artillery observer. Barrel elevation adjustments were checked using a

Right:
An immaculately restored Light Tank M5 Light Tank M5A1 in British Army markings (6th [Guards] Tank Brigade) as a Stuart VI. Note under the 53 badge is a push-out vision port for the co-driver/hull gunner. One of these was also fitted in the front (glacis) plate for the driver. *(JBn)*

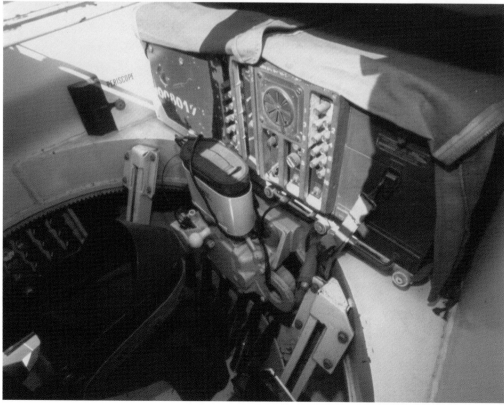

Above:
The curved armoured fairing for the turret machine gun on a restored Light Tank M5A1/Stuart VI. This cover was sometimes removed prior to operations. Note also the location of the whip aerial. *(JBn)*

Left:
Radio set No. 19 in the 'bustle' at the rear of a Stuart VI turret. Note the location of a pair of binoculars for use by the gunner or commander. *(JBn)*

hand-held Quadrant, Gunner's, M1 (known to the British as a clinometer) placed on a flat machined surface above the breech. A set of M1 Aiming Posts, for use during indirect fire missions against targets not visible from the howitzer position, was also carried.

It was appreciated that at times the howitzer might be used to deliver direct fire, typically against armoured vehicles, the gun layer had to use a Telescope M70C held in a Mount, Telescope M44. The telescope was a slight modification of the x3 magnification sight employed to aim the main gun on the M5 series light tanks.

75mm Ammunition

Being howitzers, the M2 and M3 employed a multiple charge case propellant system. The projectiles and propellant were supplied separately in cases. The propellant case contained four bags. One of these was the primary Charge 1, secured inside the case and surrounded by the primer tube which was ignited by the base-located primer being struck by the firing pin. Before loading, the correct charge to be used was determined and the appropriate number of bags (up to three) were removed from the case before the propellant and projectile were 'mated' on a special frame just prior to loading. Unwanted bags were discarded, to be disposed of later, usually by wasteful burning.

The four charges were as follows:

	Weight	Muzzle velocity	Range
Charge 1			
	.37lb	699.8ft/s	4,188 yd
	(167g)	(213m/s)	(3,830m)
Charge 2			
	.48lb	810ft/s	5,358 yd
	(218.3g)	(247m/s)	(4,900m)
Charge 3			
	.62lb	950ft/s	6,390 yd
	(280.7g)	(289.5m/s)	(6,337m)
Charge 4			
	.92lb	1,250ft/s	9,610 yd
	(416.7g)	(381m/s)	(8,787m)

The usual general purpose projectile fired from the howitzer was the Shell, High Explosive M48 (HE), identical to those fired from the series of US Army 75mm field guns dating back to World War One. The HE M48 contained 1,47lb (666g) of TNT detonated by an M48 or M51 nose fuse on impact, or by a M54 time fuse, the flight time before detonation set into the fuse before firing by a Setter, Fuze M15. With a fuse in position the HE M48 projectile weighed 14.7lb (6.67kg). At the beginning of the war these projectiles were painted yellow, although by 1945 some were olive drab.

One alternative projectile was the Shell, Chemical, M64. In appearance this resembled the HE M48. The payload for this projectile was usually 1.35lb (612g) of white phosphorus (WP) or 1.51lb (685g) of titanium chloride (FS), both creating clouds of screening or target marker smoke after impact – the contents were spread by a Tetryl-filled burster tube located along the centre of the shell interior, the grey/white smoke clouds forming rapidly as the chemical contents were exposed to the atmosphere. Also available was a Mustard (H) chemical agent

filling but this was never used operationally. Whatever the filling, at the beginning of the war these projectiles were painted a distinctive blue/grey colour, but by 1945 this had changed to grey.

For engaging armoured targets the Shell, HEAT, M66 could be fired. This differed from the other 75mm howitzer rounds in that it had a fixed propellant charge weighing .41lb (187g). The HEAT denoted High Explosive Anti-Tank, the payload being a trumpet-shaped charge (formed from 1lb [454g] of Pentolite) under the long, tapering projectile nose. On impact a M62 base fuse ignited the shaped charge to create a high-temperature jet that could rapidly travel forward through up to 3.51in (89mm) of armour at any range as the armour penetration was created using chemical energy, not kinetic energy. The projectile weight was 13.27lb (6.02kg) and had a secondary anti-personnel

capability as the projectile casing fragmented on detonation. Fired at a muzzle velocity of 1,001ft/s (305m/s), its maximum range was 4.49 miles (7,223m), although most of these projectiles were fired directly against closer range targets.

Some references also mention a Shrapnel projectile for this howitzer but it appears that none was issued operationally after 1941.

The M8 HMC had ammunition stowage for 46 rounds, sometimes augmented by the vehicle towing a further 93 rounds in an Armored Trailer M8.

As an indication of the importance of the 75mm howitzer to the US armed forces, between July 1940 and August 1945 the US artillery ammunition production facilities managed to manufacture, and deliver, a total of 26,872,000 rounds. Not all of these were for the self-propelled M8 HMC.

Above:
An M8 Howitzer Motor Carriage in action 'somewhere in the South Pacific theatre' firing at a low angle of elevation against a direct fire target. Ammunition is being unloaded from the transport tubes ready to be handed up to the gun crew in the turret. Deep wading trunking has been fitted to the hull rear. *(TM)*

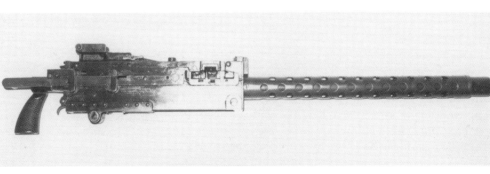

Above:
The Light Tank M5/M5A1 ball mount for the 0.30-calibre M1919A4 hull machine gun showing the box for the ammunition belt to the right of the gun and the canvas pouch for ejected cartridge cases to the left, under the gun.

Right:
The pistol grip on this 0.30-calibre machine gun denote it as a M1919A4, as used for the Light Tank M5/M5A1 hull and turret machine guns. The co-axial M1919A5 gun was identical but lacked the pistol grip and trigger as it was fired by the gunner via an electric solenoid. (TG)

Machine guns and others

The Light Tank M5 and M5A1 both carried three machine guns in addition to the main 37mm gun armament. The Combination Mount M23 and M44 both carried a co-axial 0.30-calibre M1919A5 machine gun in a fixed cradle to the right (looking forward) of the main gun. The end of the machine gun barrel protruded through the mounting shield (mantlet). The only way the M1919A5 machine differed from the other two M1919A4 guns carried was in the method of firing, via a trigger-operated solenoid, whilst it was

aimed by the gunner using the usual optical sights. All three machine guns were air-cooled and of Browning design.

One of the two 0.30-calibre M1919A4 machine guns was at the front of the vehicle in the glacis plate and operated by the co-driver. The second M1919A4 was on a pintle mounting on the turret roof. On the M5 this mounting was behind the commander's roof hatch. On the M5A1 it was relocated to the right-hand side of the turret with an armoured fairing protecting the mounting against damage. (The fairing was often removed.)

Each of these guns had a cyclic fire rate of 400 to 500 rounds-per-minute (rpm) with

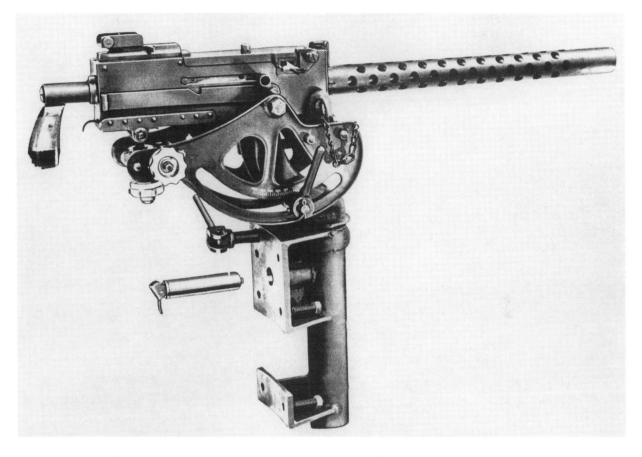

ammunition fed in belts of variable capacity but usually holding 250 rounds. The pre-filled belts were stowed in metal boxes around the interior of the fighting compartment, the M5 carrying an 'official' 6,250 rounds, the M5A1 a total of 6,500 rounds. Each of the machine guns weighed about 30.9lb (14kg). Also carried on the vehicle was a Tripod M2 for dismounted use with the commander's machine gun.

Each M5 also had provision to carry one 0.45-calibre sub-machine gun, again for dismounted or close-in defensive purposes. This weapon was originally a M1928, M1 or M1A1, all variations of the Thompson or 'Tommy Gun'. Later in the war there came the Gun, Submachine Caliber 0.45, M3 or M3A1, the infamous 'Grease Gun'. The M5 carried 420 pistol rounds for the M3/M3A1 - in the M5A1 a total of 540 rounds were carried for the same weapon.

Also carried on each vehicle were 12 hand grenades. These comprised four Fragmentation Mk II, two Offensive Mk III, four Smoke HC M8, and two Thermite Incendiary. The latter was intended to be used to destroy the interior to prevent the tank falling into enemy hands in a usable state.

On the M8 Howitzer Motor Carriage the main defensive weapon was a single 0.50-calibre Machine Gun M2 HB (HB - heavy barrel) mounted on a pintle at the rear of the turret. This air-cooled, heavy machine gun had a cyclic fire rate of from 450 to 600 rpm, with rounds fed into the gun in disintegrating metal link belts. The M2 HB weighed a hefty 83.8lb (38kg). Ammunition belt lengths could be varied at will but usually held 50 rounds. In the M8 HMC a total of 400 rounds of .50-calibre ammunition was carried stowed in boxes each of 50 rounds.

Also carried on each M8 HMC was a 0.45-calibre sub-machine gun, as with the Light Tank M5. Stowage for 600 rounds of .45 ammunition was provided. In addition the crew also had access to three 0.30-calibre Carbines M1 for personal defence or dismounted fighting. A total of 735 rounds were provided for these Carbines, the ammunition being of a different type from the 0.30 machine gun rounds. In addition to all these items there were eight hand grenades, two of each of the same types as carried in the light tank.

Above:
The turret machine gun mounting for a Light Tank M5/M5A1 showing how it was secured to the right-hand side of the turret. The arc mounting under the gun allowed a considerable degree of barrel elevation for air defence, although this operation often had to be carried out from outside the turret.

CHAPTER FOUR

VARIANTS

Compared to many other armoured vehicles in service between 1939 and 1945, the number of variants based on the Light Tank M5 and M5A1 was relatively low. Although most of these were little more than turretless vehicles, the main variant was the widely deployed M8 (HMC) self-propelled howitzer.

The numerically commonest variant based on the Light Tank M5 series was the M8 Howitzer Motor Carriage (HMC). In early 1941 a request was officially recognised for a close-support artillery vehicle to operate at medium tank battalion headquarters level. One immediate response was the mounting of a 75mm Pack Howitzer M1A1 behind a shield on a suitably modified M3 half-track, the Howitzer Motor Carriage T30. This proposal was soon regarded as only partly satisfactory for co-operation with medium tanks as, apart from an overall lack of armoured protection for the howitzer and its crew, plus some other disadvantages, the half-tracked chassis lacked the cross-country performance that a fully tracked platform could provide. (However, 500 examples of the T30 were manufactured by International Harvester of Chicago during 1942.) Consideration therefore switched to utilising the Light Tank M5. It was considered that the M5 engine installation could deliver sufficient power to accommodate the additional weight of the howitzer and its ammunition, and it was already available on the production lines.

Ordnance Department engineers at Aberdeen Proving Ground accordingly constructed the Howitzer Motor Carriage T41, a trials mock-up using an M5 chassis and with a limited-traverse 75mm howitzer mounted in a raised front plate. To provide more internal space the hull was widened. As it was considered that the howitzer installation lacked sufficient protection for the vehicle interior, and the wider hull would introduce complications on the production lines, this approach was soon abandoned in favour of another proposal. This time the intention was to mount the howitzer in a new open-topped turret (sometimes referred to as a semi-turret) placed directly onto an only slightly modified M5 hull. The result became the Howitzer Motor Carriage T41.

On 23 April 1942 the T41 was type classified as the M8 Howitzer Motor Carriage, production commencing during September that year and lasting until January 1944. A total of 1,778 examples were manufactured, all by the Cadillac Motor Car Division of the General Motors Corporation in Detroit. During 1942 only 373 examples were produced. In 1943, total production was 1,330 and the last 75 were completed in January 1944. The M8 HMC first saw combat in Italy during mid-1943. Thereafter it served in all U.S Army theatres of war.

Above:
A pilot model of the M8 Howitzer Motor Carriage undergoing mobility trials. Note the vehicle is fitted with sand shields. Also the vehicle's Vertical Volute Suspension (VVS) can be clearly seen. *(TM)*

Left:
A pilot example of the M8 Howitzer Motor Carriage with the 0.50 M2 heavy machine gun in position clearly shows the driver and co-driver's access and vision hatches now relocated to the hull front (glacis) plate. *(TM)*

Above:
Not always apparent in illustrations of the M8 Howitzer Motor Carriage is how open the turret really was, often being referred to as a semi-turret. The space taken up by the 75mm howitzer inside the turret can be readily appreciated, as can the close proximity of the 0.50-calibre M2 heavy machine gun mounting. *(TM)*

Right:
An M8 Howitzer Motor Carriage moving past a Jeep column. *(TM)*

With an enlarged rear overhang, the cast steel turret was larger than the usual 37mm gun equivalent so the driver's and co-driver's access/escape hatches had to be moved to the sloping front plate. This change was necessitated by the enlarged turret having the advantage of a full 360° traverse so it partially overlapped the locations of the usual M5 superstructure roof hatches. The front hull machine gun was also eliminated. Apart from internal stowage arrangements for 46 rounds and the provision of one 0.50-calibre M2 HB machine gun mounting over the turret for air and local defence, that was just about all that was necessary to change the M5 from a light tank to an artillery platform. The installation of the larger turret and howitzer meant that the vehicle's combat weight increased to 15.42 tons (15,670kg), as opposed to about 14.73 tons (14,970kg) for the M5. There was no change from the usual overall height and the crew strength remained at four, the co-driver doubling as an extra loader for the howitzer.

As it was felt that internal ammunition stowage capacity (46 rounds) was somewhat limited, it was sometimes augmented by towing a further 93 rounds carried in an Armored Trailer M8. This trailer was manufactured by John Deere & Company and was considered to be an awkward load, resulting in its use being strictly limited.

As a footnote, the turret and its 75mm howitzer were also employed on the US Marine Corps' Landing, Vehicle, Tracked, (Armored), LVT(A)-4 and LVT(A)-5.

Details of the 75mm howitzer, its ammunition and other M8-associated weapons are described in Chapter 4 (see page 49).

By late 1944 the M8 HMC was being gradually phased out of service in favour of the longer ranged and more effective 105mm howitzer mounted on the M7 Howitzer Motor Carriage, but when the war ended the M8 HMC was still in service.

An Ordnance listing dated October 1947 mentioned the M8 HMC as still likely to be encountered in US Army artillery parks, no doubt most of them serving with National Guard units. The type had not featured in the usual Lend-Lease Programme lists but, with the war

(cont page 63)

Above:
An M8 Howitzer Motor Carriage crew undergoing final training prior to the D-Day landings, 6 June 1944. The barrel elevation is positioned for direct fire, although higher elevations were more often used to allow plunging fire onto enemy targets. *(TM)*

Above:
Part of a battery of M8 Howitzer Motor Carriages undergoing training somewhere in southern England during 1944 and showing no inclination to use normal dispersal and camouflage procedures against air attack. *(TM)*

Right:
Despite all the attempts to disguise this vehicle under foliage the turret of an M8 Howitzer Motor Carriage betrays its presence. *(TM)*

Above:
A fully-laden M8 Howitzer Motor Carriage in action somewhere in Europe during late 1944, with extra sandbag protection added to the front hull. Also visible is the rudimentary nature of the crew's personal kit stowage and the weather cover over the machine gun. *(TM)*

Left:
An illustration from a series of ballistic test programmes undertaken during 1942 and intended to fully explore the possibilities of the 75mm Howitzer M1A1 in its then novel M8 Howitzer Motor Carriage turret. *(TG)*

Above and right:
As far as is known only a single prototype of the Howitzer Motor Carriage Modified, or M8A1, was produced. It was a combination of a Howitzer Motor Carriage M8 hull, a modified M8 turret and a 75mm Gun M3 as employed on the early Medium Tank M4 series. It was apparently devised to produce a light tank destroyer. Very little appears to have been recorded regarding this vehicle but it was apparently not a success, no doubt being cramped and top heavy. *(TM)*

over, examples were passed to many nations, especially in Central and South America. The French Army was one European user. Numbers of M8s HMC were still in service with Mexico until (at least) the mid-1970s.

Howitzer Motor Carriage T82

In December 1943 there began one further effort to utilise the M5 light tank series as a self-propelled artillery vehicle, this time to act as a self-propelled artillery platform to operate in the close confines of jungle warfare in the Pacific theatre. For this role a short-barrelled 105mm M3 howitzer, having a maximum possible range of 8,295yd (7,585m) when firing a 33lb (14.97kg) high-explosive projectile, was located on a limited traverse mounting in the front plate of an open, raised superstructure built over the M5 chassis. Internal ammunition stowage provision was made for 58 rounds. This was the Howitzer Motor Carriage T82; two examples were produced for trials.

It appears that the intention was to convert redundant M5s for the T82's jungle fighting role, rather than manufacture new vehicles. The crew was four and the combat weight about 14.27 tons (14,500kg). By May 1945 it had been decided that there was no longer any need for a specialised vehicle such as the T82; the project was cancelled.

Mortars

During 1943 the US Army made a request for a prototype mobile mortar carriage designed to support mechanised infantry units. The M5A1 was one vehicle selected for trials, the initial result being the 81mm Mortar Motor Carriage (MMC) T27. For this the M5A1 turret was removed and an open-topped super-structure added – the superstructure was formed from armoured plates about 17.73in (450mm) high and .98in (25mm) thick. The mortar involved was the standard US medium calibre infantry mortar used throughout the

Above:
Intended for jungle warfare in the Pacific theatre, the Howitzer Motor Carriage T82, armed with a 105mm Howitzer M3, was overtaken by events as, with the end of the war in sight, the project was terminated in May 1945. *(TM)*

Above:
The 81mm Mobile Mortar Carriage T27 was based on a Light Tank M5A1 hull with a raised superstructure to house an elevated mortar firing forward from the open interior. Early trials demonstrated that the interior was too small to carry a mortar crew with a viable amount of ammunition so the project was cancelled during April 1944. *(TM)*

Right:
The raised superstructure of the 81mm Mobile Mortar Carriage T27 can be appreciated from this view, as can its proposed secondary armament of two 0.50-calibre M2 heavy machine guns. *(TM)*

Left:
The addition of a 7.2in T39 rocket launcher to the turret of a Light Tank M5 appears to have been experimental. The launcher traversed with the turret while a direct connection to the main gun barrel altered elevation. The T39 did not enter production. *(TM)*

war years. It was an 81mm M1 firing a 6.88lb (3.12kg) bomb to a maximum range of just over 3,290yd (3,010m). It was secured to fire forward over a traverse arc of 35°. A 0.50-calibre M2 HB heavy machine gun was also provided on a pintle mounting. An alternative design with the mortar tube set lower in the vehicle, the T27E1, was also devised but trials with the T27 soon demonstrated that the interior of the M5A1 was too limited to accommodate the mortar, its crew of two or three and a viable ammunition load. The T27 and T27E1 were therefore cancelled in April 1944, the 81mm Mortar Motor Carriage role being assumed by half-tracks.

Not deterred by the conclusion of the T27 mobile mortar programme, it was soon followed by an attempt to install an even larger 4.2in (107mm) rifled mortar instead. This resulted in the 4.2in Mortar Motor Carriage T29.

The mortar area was enlarged slightly but it still remained too restricted for comfort and the available ammunition stowage space proved insufficient, so that programme was also abandoned.

Rockets

As far as can be determined the M5 was involved with only one series of artillery rocket trials, conducted during 1944. The rocket launcher involved was the T39 carrying twenty 7.2in (183mm) rockets with a maximum possible range of almost 1,200yd (1,100m) - operational ranges would have been shorter. The T39 consisted of a flat steel box with two rows of ten launcher rails, one above the other. Carried on an elevating frame over the turret, the launcher box was connected by an arm leading to a bracket on the main gun barrel. Altering the gun barrel elevation also altered the launcher box elevation. Traversing the turret also traversed the launcher box. It seems that only one M5 tank was so equipped, probably for feasibility trials – but these were not continued.

Above:
A single prototype of a Light Tank M5A1 with an E9-9 flame gun positioned on the hull front was produced in trials form only. Much of the fuel and propellant gas for the flame gun were carried in a vulnerable looking towed trailer. *(TM)*

Right:
A Light Tank M5A1 carrying an E7-7 flame gun in place of the main armament was under preparation for the invasion of Japan. But the war ended and it was never used in action. *(TM)*

Flamethrowers

The Light Tank M5 series carried over the same role of mechanised flamethrower as the Light Tank M3 series. Few examples actually saw action as the Ordnance Department was reluctant to divert tanks for flame warfare, despite calls from the US Army and Marine Corps for such equipments. With the M5A1 the most numerous application was with the E7-7 Flame-gun, with a short flamethrower tube taking the place of the turret 37mm gun armament. Flame fuel was carried internally in a tank with a capacity of 87.34gals (397ltr), with the necessary compressed propellant gas in pressure bottles stowed in the turret bustle. The fuel could be discharged at the rate of 1.65gals (7.5ltr) every second. Maximum effective range using standard flame fuel was between 88.6 and 118ft (27 and 36m). By using a special thickened fuel the range could be increased to 311.7/393.4ft (95/120m). It is understood that some M5A1 vehicles carrying the E7-7 were being prepared for the invasion of the Japanese mainland when the war ended.

Two further mechanised flamethrower projects concerning the M5A1 remained at the

prototype stage. In January 1943 the E8 equipment was tested. This involved removing the turret from the M5A1 and building a box-type superstructure over the turret ring. The E8 flamethrower tube was located in a small traversing turret on top of the superstructure.

For the E9-9 flamethrower equipment the flame projector was fitted on the hull front, the main gun armament being retained. The flame fuel was towed behind the M5A1 in what looked like an extremely vulnerable and easily identifiable singe-axle trailer, with an armoured pipe carrying the fuel to the tank interior. Only one example was produced.

Obstacles

One simple variation for clearing battlefield obstacles and preparing artillery or combat vehicle field positions was the installation of a dozer blade at the front of an M5 series light tank. This combat engineer measure was introduced in limited numbers during 1944. For this role some vehicles had their turrets removed.

The M5/M5A1 was one of the vehicles fitted with the Culin Prong, or Culin Hedgerow Device (also known as Rhinoceros). This was a field expedient devised by one Sergeant Culin

Right:
The Culin Hedgerow Device was fitted as a field expedient. There were several slightly differing forms but all were manufactured and installed at field workshops in France using steel from cleared German beach obstacles. Note also the sandbags added to provide stand-off protection against German shaped-charge warheads. *(TM)*

Right:
A Culin Hedgerow Device carried on a Light Tank M5 in Northern France, late June 1944. The devices removed thick hedgerows purely by driving against them at speed, the prongs cutting their way through dense vegetation. *(TM)*

during late June 1944 as a means of removing the formidable obstacles presented by the ancient and dense hedgerows widely encountered throughout the close confines of the Bocage area of Normandy. Getting combat vehicles through the hedgerows was normally a risky and awkward task (there was also the danger of well-camouflaged enemy tank-killer troops) until Sergeant Culin devised a horizontal array of steel teeth, or prongs, that were welded or otherwise secured to the lower front of Allied tanks. All the installations were carried out at field workshops or similar facilities, the steel coming from cleared German beach obstacles. In use, the carrier tank simply drove towards the hedgerow to be breached at the highest speed possible, the force of the impact cutting through or uprooting the blocking vegetation and allowing the tank to pass through rapidly. Once the Bocage country was left behind by the rapid Allied advances of late July and August 1944 the Culin device was usually removed.

Reconnaissance

Turretless M5 and M5A1 light tanks were both utilised as reconnaissance vehicles. Although turreted light tanks were also widely used in this role, removing the turret lowered the profile considerably, while the reduced overall weight of the vehicle enabled higher top speeds to be reached. As armoured reconnaissance relied on vehicles getting away from potential trouble fast, while making the maximum use of available cover, reducing the overall silhouette made good sense. Reconnaissance troops equipped with the M5 or M5A1 knew that their 37mm gun armament was of little combat utility so the lack

Left:
The Reconnaissance Vehicle T8E1 was simply a turretless Light Tank M5 or M5A1 with a machine gun ring installed over the former turret ring. This considerably lowered the overall height of the vehicle, rendering it more suitable for the reconnaissance role. *(TM)*

Above:
Although the command and liaison versions of the turretless Light Tank M5/M5A1 had no official designation (sometimes referred to as the T5 Command Tank) they were readily identifiable by the open box-type turret. This example was used by Brigadier-General George Read, assistant divisional commander of the US Army's 6th Armored Division, 1945. *(TM)*

Right:
The Reconnaissance Vehicle T8E1 with spare track shoes and grousers (spuds) stowed on the front hull. *(TM)*

of a turret mattered little. Machine guns were mounted as defence armament.

Many units removed the turrets in the field as a locally introduced expedient. During 1944 redundant M5/M5A1 chassis were 'officially' so converted with the introduction of the Reconnaissance Vehicle T8, a limited standard vehicle. After 'conversion' a ring mounting for one (sometimes two) 0.50-calibre M2 HB heavy machine gun was positioned on the former turret ring. A tarpaulin cover was usually carried to keep out the worst effects of the weather.

To extend the capabilities of this conversion a number of T8s were issued in T8E1 form, the differences being that the T8E1 had extra stowage racks plus further racks along each side, all to carry anti-tank mines and a lower machine gun ring.

Command

Command or liaison versions of the M5 and M5A1 were created along the same lines as for the reconnaissance vehicles. The turret was removed and the interior then fitted-out to carry extra radio equipment, map tables and other command equipment. Most examples had a raised open box superstructure to provide extra protection for the occupants. The British Army used its Stuart VI vehicles extensively in the command role.

Personnel carriers

The use of turretless M5 and M5A1 light tanks as armoured personnel carriers was very much a British and Canadian expedient, generally known as the Kangaroo. The Kangaroo concept was introduced during 1943 using M7 (Priest) self-propelled howitzers (with main gun removed) or turretless Ram tanks, with seating provided in the interior for infantry. The concept also extended to turretless M5 and M5A1s, although the available seating space was limited to about six

(cont page 76)

Above:
A superbly restored example of a turretless Light Tank M5/M5A1 in Kangaroo armoured personnel carrier form. Details are correct down to the stowage of grousers (spuds) on the front (glacis) plate. In combat the Kangaroo could carry six fully-equipped troops and driver. *(JBn)*

Above:
The British Army made frequent use of its Stuart VI light tanks by removing the turret and using them as anti-tank gun tractors, this North African example towing a 17-pounder anti-tank gun and manned by a crew from a Scottish regiment. *(TM)*

Right:
Turretless Stuart VI light tanks were often used as reconnaissance vehicles by British Army units. This example is provided with a canvas roof cover to provide some protection against Italian weather. *(TM)*

Above:
A turretless Stuart VI light tank being put to good use as a tractor for a 17-pounder anti-tank gun during operations in North Africa, 1943. Note the white cross on the side of the vehicle as an extra aid to field recognition. *(TM)*

Left:
An unusual illustration of a turretless Light Tank M5 series armoured personnel carrier in service with the Egyptian Army during the early postwar years. *(TM)*

Right:
A fully-equipped late series M5A1 at a battle re-enactment show. This restored vehicle is painted in late D-Day colours: olive drab, white stars and white unit/vehicle identifying symbols and numbers. *(JBn)*

Above:
A Psy-war Light Tank
M5A1 equipped with
an AN-UIQ-1 public
address system over
the turret, operating
in Germany during
latter days of the
war. This variant
retained its main
armament, further
protection against
short-range shaped-
charge projectiles
being provided by
the addition of
sandbags. (TM)

soldiers, at the most. The British Army retained its light tank Kangaroos for some years after 1945.

Amphibious

In common with many other Allied armoured vehicles the M5/M5A1 was considered as suitable for amphibious warfare - as long as appropriate kits were available. Several such conversion kits were considered and tested, most involving extensive sealing of all hatches and engine access points, together with raised

ventilation/exhaust ducts for the engine. Unlike kits for the M3 series, none was officially adopted for service as by the time their main application would have arisen (June 1944) the main US Army tank warfare burden had been allocated to the M4 (Sherman) series. In the Pacific theatre the US Marine Corps relied on its Landing, Vehicle, Tracked (Armoured) LVT(A).

Psy-war

Perhaps the most unusual employment of the M5A1 was as a carrier for Psy-war

equipment. Introduced during late 1944 this was simply a standard M5A1, complete with gun and turret, carrying loudspeakers and/or public address equipment (such as the AN-UIQ-1) on the turret roof. The loudspeakers were used to broadcast news programmes and propaganda towards the enemy front lines, the objective being to lower morale of German troops or civilians and discourage any further fighting.

The M5 and M5A1 featured in many trials programmes, many of them with no direct application for the M5 light tank series, the vehicles being used purely as trials platforms. Many of these trials related to automotive or armament developments, typical of the latter being a twin 0.30-calibre low-level air defence machine gun installation. This vehicle never entered production as it lacked the necessary firepower.

Another armament project to which reference has been found involved the fitting of an automatic 37mm gun, again almost certainly for air defence. The only likely candidate for this role would have been a suitably modified 37mm Automatic Gun M1, a light anti-aircraft gun, but this weapon would have almost certainly proved to be too powerful for the M5/M5A1 chassis. Few details of this project appear to have survived.

Above:
The Light Tank M5A1 remains a popular vehicle for combat vehicle restorers and military enthusiasts with many examples surviving in private hands, such as this M5A1 resident in England. It is well provided with the late 1944 clutter of extra stowage and even a Culin Hedgerow Device. *(JBn)*

Right:
Close-up detail of a Light Tank M5A1 drive sprocket and Vertical Volute Suspension (VVS) system unit. *(JBn)*

Above:
The restorer of this pristine Light Tank M5A1 has gone to great lengths not only to keep the vehicle running but has added finishing details such as gun covers and other stowage. *(JBn)*

Left:
The rear-idler wheel of a Light Tank M5A1 and the trailing link suspension arm, also a feature of the earlier M3 series. *(JBn)*

Above:
Several attempts were made to render the Light Tank M5/M5A1 suitable for amphibious operations, this example being one of the more complicated trial versions with air intake and engine exhaust housings at the rear and extensive side skirts for the tracks. *(TG)*

Right:
An exhaust housing intended to be fitted to the rear of a Light Tank M5/M5A1 for amphibious operations. There were many similar trial structures, most of them destined never to be used. *(TM)*

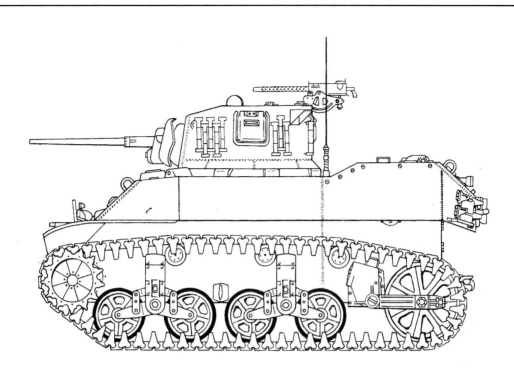

M5
Side view and internal section. (Scale 1:35)

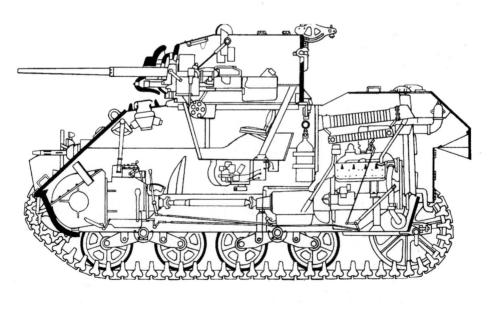

© 2004 DP. Dyer.

Stuart VI (M5A1)
in British service, Operation Torch, North Africa, 1942

© 2004 Mike Rose.

M5 70th Independent Tank Battalion,
Casablanca, Morocco, November 1942

© 2001 Mike Rose.

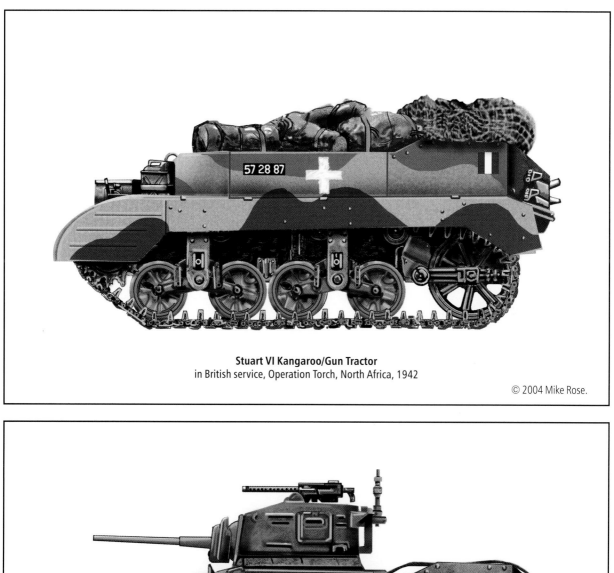

Stuart VI Kangaroo/Gun Tractor
in British service, Operation Torch, North Africa, 1942

© 2004 Mike Rose.

M5
Operation Torch, North Africa, 1942

© 2004 Mike Rose.

Right:
German civilians
witnessing the
advance of a well-
laden US Army Light
Tank M5A1 unit
during the very last
days of operations in
March 1945. *(TM)*

M8 Howitzer Motor Carriage
Free French Army, Division Blindée

© 2004 Mike Rose.

M8 Howitzer Motor Carriage
Free French Army, Division Blindée

© 2004 Mike Rose.

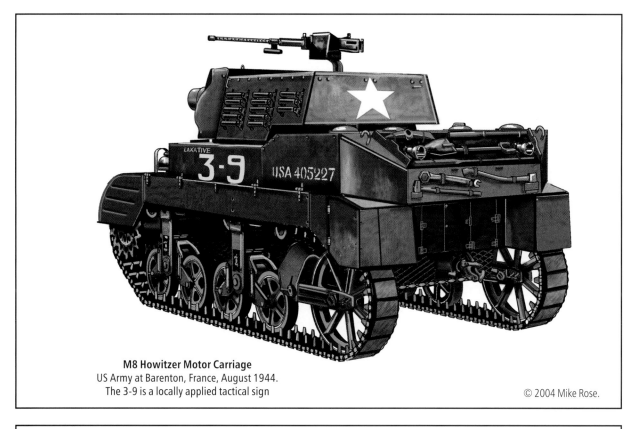

M8 Howitzer Motor Carriage
US Army at Barenton, France, August 1944.
The 3-9 is a locally applied tactical sign

© 2004 Mike Rose.

M8 Howitzer Motor Carriage
106th Cavalry Reconnaissance Group, February 1945

© 2004 Mike Rose.

CHAPTER FIVE

PRODUCTION

The main feature of the M5 series production story is that production continued long after it was apparent that the design's combat shortcomings were to limit tactical applications. But as long as the established production lines could readily produce vehicles, good use could be made of the M5, even if only to make up numbers.

As soon as the Light Tank M5 Cadillac engine configuration was type classified in February 1942 work began to establish a production line at the Cadillac facility at Detroit, Illinois. The line was established as Cadillac automobile manufacture was ceasing due to the war. By 1942 the market prospects for the usual Cadillac prestige products had almost disappeared and the marque had not been selected to supply the demand for military staff cars.

The first Cadillac-built M5 rolled off the Detroit production line in March 1942, having been virtually hand built direct from drawings. Such was the rush to production that the manufacturing jigs and gauges were still being made when the first vehicles were completed. The production line had to carry on running without these items. Concurrent with this rush to production was a shortage of suitable machine tools, so numerous existing manufacturers in the Detroit area became involved in the supply of the many and various M5 components.

Such was the demand for the M5 and light tanks generally that a Cadillac plant at Southgate, California was established as a second production centre, the first examples from that line appearing during July 1942.

It was not long before yet more production facilities were established. Once again with Cadillac assistance, the Massey-Harris agricultural machine manufacturer took over the unused Nash-Kelvinator plant at Racine, Wisconsin, as another M5 assembly plant. To add to the swelling totals, in September-October 1943 the American Car & Foundry plant at Berwick, Pennsylvania, became involved. Until then building the Light Tank M3A3, it simply switched production to the Light Tank M5A1 with hardly a break and continued to manufacture the type until the last one rolled off the production line in June 1944. The M5A1 replaced the M5 on the production lines in February 1943.

Production of the last M5A1 was completed during June 1944. Until then the annual totals from all production centres were as follows:

1942	2,858
1943	4,063
1944	1,963
Total	8,884.

Of this total, 6,810 were the M5A1 model.

In the rush to M5 production many counter-productive short-term measures were adopted and delays were caused by the erratic supply of

[cont page 92]

Above:
US Army Light Tank M5A1s advancing through a German town in the latter days of the war in 1945, the commanders being ready with their turret machine guns in case of trouble. *(TA)*

Left:
M8 Howitzer Motor Carriages in southern England prior to embarking on LSTs for deployment in northern Europe. *(TM)*

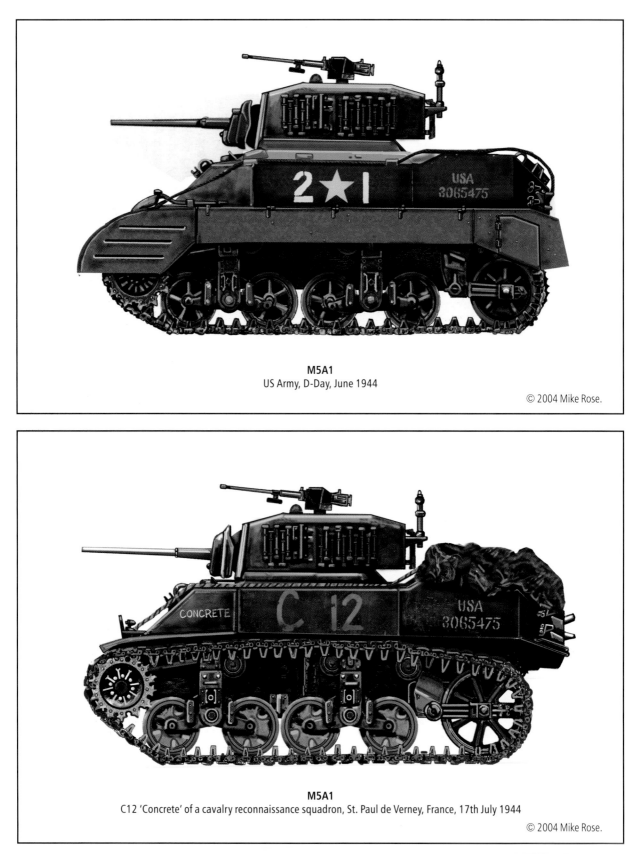

M5A1
US Army, D-Day, June 1944

© 2004 Mike Rose.

M5A1
C12 'Concrete' of a cavalry reconnaissance squadron, St. Paul de Verney, France, 17th July 1944

© 2004 Mike Rose.

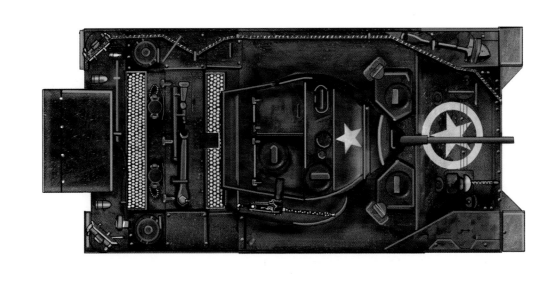

M5A1
11th Armoured Battalion, Germany, 1945

© 2004 Mike Rose.

M5A1
11th Armoured Battalion, Germany, 1945

© 2004 Mike Rose.

important components, to say nothing of missing small items that had to be included to make a newly-manufactured combat vehicle operational. At first this meant that almost-completed vehicles had to be stockpiled in parks outside their production centres awaiting the supply of missing items, sometimes for periods lasting weeks. During one period in 1942 it was tracks that were in particularly short supply. The sight of so many vehicles lined up and doing nothing had a depressing effect on production personnel morale as it seemed their labours to rapidly produce

vehicles at the rates requested were being wasted at a time when their products were badly needed by the troops at the battlefront.

Many of the supply delays were actually the responsibility of the Ordnance Department rather than the manufacturer, so it assumed the task of equipping and finally preparing the completed vehicles for shipment overseas. This was carried out at a series of Tank Depots to which the newly assembled vehicles were transported. Once there the vehicles could be stored until all the many items such as radios, first

Left:
Among the last preparations for the June 1944 D-Day landings was the loading of vehicles, in this case Light Tank M5A1s, onto Diamond-T tank transporters to carry them from delivery ports to locations on the south coast of England. The examples shown are not equipped for amphibious operations and each carries crates of combat spares over the engine compartment. *(TM)*

aid kits and all the various spare equipment needed to make the vehicle combat-ready could be installed, and made ready for shipment.

The first Tank Depot was established at Toledo, Ohio, in early January 1942. The Electric Auto-Lite Company took over and ran the New York Central Railroad workshops in the town as an interim measure until more suitable facilities could be found. Two further Tank Depots were soon established by the Ford Motor Company at its assembly plants at Chester, Pennsylvania, and Richmond, California. In December 1942 a proposed artillery manufacturing plant at Lima, Ohio, was converted to a Tank Depot under the control of the United Motors Service Division of General Motors. Operations at the Toledo depot then ceased.

Another Tank Depot was established at Montreal, Canada specifically to cater for the different equipment needs of Lend–Lease Programme vehicles for delivery to British and Commonwealth armed forces. Known as the Longue Pointe depot, it was run by the Canadian Army.

M5A1
Germany, 1945. Note the Battalion marking

© 2004 Mike Rose.

M5A1
US Marine Corps, Pacific 1944.
(machine gun removed for jungle fighting)

© 2004 Mike Rose.

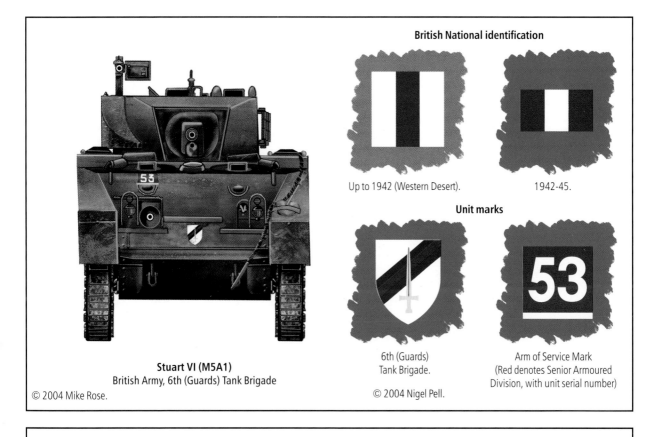

Stuart VI (M5A1)
British Army, 6th (Guards) Tank Brigade

© 2004 Mike Rose.

British National identification

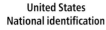

Up to 1942 (Western Desert).

1942-45.

Unit marks

6th (Guards)
Tank Brigade.

© 2004 Nigel Pell.

Arm of Service Mark
(Red denotes Senior Armoured
Division, with unit serial number)

United States
National identification

Tank turret usage.

Allied air recognition signs.

Allied air recognition.

Allied air recognition, variant.

Variant, ordered before
the invasion of Sicily.

French National identification

National Identification Mark,
North Africa.

National Identification Mark from
late 1943.

National Identification Mark
variant, from late 1943.

French Divisional insignia,Cross of Lorraine
variants appear in several Divisions.

© 2004 Nigel Pell.

Above: A Stuart VI of the British Army's 6th (Guards) Tank Brigade. The censor has removed the white shield emblem of the Brigade. *(TM)*